GEOPHYSICAL MONOGRAPH SERIES

Ian Jones, managing editor

NUMBER 15

The Misadventures of Interpreter Sam

Donald A. Herron

Illustrated by David Carman

Society of Exploration Geophysicists
The international society of applied geophysics
Tulsa, Oklahoma, U.S.A.

ISBN 978-0-931830-56-3 (Series)
ISBN 978-1-56080-156-6 (Volume)

Society of Exploration Geophysicists
P.O. Box 702740
Tulsa, OK 74170-2740

© 2009 by Society of Exploration Geophysicists
All rights reserved. This book or parts hereof may not be reproduced in any form without written permission from the publisher.

Published 2009
Printed in the United States of America

Library of Congress Cataloging-in-Publication Data

Herron, Donald A., 1949-
 The misadventures of interpreter Sam / Donald A. Herron ; illustrated by David Carman.
    p. cm. -- (Geophysical monograph series)
  Includes bibliographical references.
  ISBN 978-1-56080-156-6 (alk. paper)
  1. Seismic prospecting--Humor. 2. Geophysical surveys--Humor.
 3. Geophysicists--Vocational guidance--Humor. I. Title.

TN269.H465 2009
622'.1592--dc22

2009024210

For the Sam in all of us

Contents

About the Author	vii
Acknowledgments	viii
Introduction	ix

Chapter 1: Precursors 1
    Where it began 2
    What we do 3
    If Charles Dickens had been an interpreter 4
    Characteristics of an interpreter 5

Chapter 2: 2003 7
    How much data can an interpreter pick 8
    I need a regional map by tomorrow morning 10
    Move your pick down, move your pick up 12
    Memories of mentors 14
    Seeing green that wasn't there before 16
    The horde of peons that make maps 17

Chapter 3: 2004 19
    A visit from home 20
    Finding the perfect match 21
    Becoming another Fred Henning 23
    Measuring success 26
    Remembering Dad's advice 28
    Examining staff's handiwork 30

Chapter 4: 2005 33
    Jim Patch's poetry 34
    Finrus and the Block 289 farm-out 36
    Verifying preconceived notions 38
    The best meeting ever 40
    John's checking my ties 42
    You're not interpreting fast enough 44
    If the structure were there, it would have been found
        long ago 47

Chapter 5: 2006 49
    One map for us, another for the partners 50
    Sam visits the 2005 Annual Meeting 52
    Demurkifying data 54
    The trip to the construction yard 56
    The morning paper and Sergeant Jimmy Hall 58
    If the fault is there, then I've missed thousands more
        like it 60

Chapter 6: 2007 63
    Marginal versus considerable 64
    Sam returns to New Orleans 66
    The top secret Technology Innovation Award 68
    The evolution of the new-hire field trip 70
    Paul's exit interview 73
    Mistakes on the slides 75
    Sam visits San Antonio 77

Chapter 7: 2008 81
    The offer he couldn't refuse 82
    Right at the wrong time 84
    How to get a workstation upgrade 86
    Criticizing other interpreters 88
    The best interpreter in the company 90

Epilogue 93

Suggested Reading 95

About the Author

Don Herron has enjoyed a career as a seismic interpreter at Texaco (1973–1977), Gulf (1977–1984), and most recently Sohio/BP (1984–2008). At both Gulf and Sohio/BP he taught in-house courses in seismic interpretation and was coinstructor for the SEG public course "Seismic Interpretation in the Exploration Domain" from 1995 to 2007. He was chairman of the SEG Continuing Education Committee (1998–2001) and a member of the Editorial Board of THE LEADING EDGE (2002–2007, chairman in 2006–2007). Herron currently is chairman of the SEG Interpretation Committee. He is an active member of SEG, AAPG, and Sigma Xi, and he always has taken the time to observe and write about the world around him. ▶

Acknowledgments

Thanks to my love Rosemary for bearing with my rehashing of Sam's stories time and again at the dinner table, to THE LEADING EDGE editor Dean Clark for taking a chance on Sam, to the SEG staff in Tulsa, especially Ted Bakamjian, Jennifer Cobb, Kathy Gamble, and Linda Adams, and to David Carman, Sam's illustrator, for applying their many talents to make this book a reality, to C. H. Dix for encouraging me many years ago when I most needed it, and to countless fellow interpreters for providing the camaraderie that has brought Sam to life. ▶

—Don Herron
April 2009

Introduction

Sam was born early in 2003 after a gestation period covering the four or five months leading up to the start of my first year on the Editorial Board of THE LEADING EDGE (*TLE*). I conceived him as an individual through whom I could tell stories based on the broad range of my own experiences and those of interpreters I've known over 35 years in the oil and gas industry. Sam is a composite of these men and women—not a Frankenstein, but a kaleidoscopic Everyman, as he is referred to in the subtitle to the bimonthly feature in *TLE* that bears his name. At its center, each of Sam's stories contains a kernel of truth, and some are hybrids of several truths, but I would misrepresent him if I didn't admit to having embellished some of his escapades, if not actually having engaged in high flights of fancy in relating them.

The order of Sam's stories in this book is the chronological sequence in which they were published in *TLE*, which, with one or two exceptions, reflects the order in which I wrote them. I had no particular plan or progression of ideas in mind as I wrote these stories, and if anything their order represents only the unregulated and unpredictable flow of my memories. I've also given each story a title of sorts that didn't appear with its original version.

With conviction I can say that in all of his comings and goings Sam never has intended to bash anyone or anything in our industry. Rather, through his stories he observes what we do and comments accordingly, and therein is the context for reading about him—nothing more, nothing less. ▶

Chapter 1: Precursors

Where it began

There are three contributions to *TLE* that I consider to be precursors to Interpreter Sam. The first of these is, of all things, a poem titled "What we do" that appeared in the Interpreter's Corner feature in the May 1996 issue. I wrote this verse, which on a good day meets the definition of doggerel, after having spent many hours on many different occasions preparing prospect presentations for management. The second is a short piece titled "If Charles Dickens had been an interpreter" that was published in the December 2002 issue. In this article I transformed part of a conversation between the Ghost of Christmas Present and Ebenezer Scrooge in Dickens's *A Christmas Carol* from its 19th century setting into the 21st century. My motivation for writing this story, patterned very closely after the actual structure of the original Dickens, came from the frustration of dealing with disk space limitations on my own workstation, being especially mindful of the play on words between "prisons and workhouses" and "disk space and workstations." The third is an article titled "Characteristics of an interpreter" that was published in the January 2003 issue, immediately preceding the issue in which the first Interpreter Sam column appeared. This article includes a list of the professional and personal qualities that interpreters might ideally have, and readers should be assured that in compiling this list I purposely mixed the humorous with the serious. In writing these latter two articles, I decided that the best method for offering comments about our profession would be through the tradition of storytelling, which in the case of Sam involves a not-so-fictitious character who openly invites other interpreters and all readers to share not only what he does but also how and why he does it. ❧

What we do

MAY 1996

We looked at our maps, and saw they were wrong
There were contours and faults where they didn't belong
But we took them to drafting, nevertheless,
And a prospect they forged from the unholy mess.

We sent our work to The Chief for review
He attacked with red pencil, and when he was through
What had been our top prospect, refined and polished,
Lay torn, fragmented, completely demolished.

Experience had taught us not to be surprised
By this turn of events, and we soon realized
What had to be done—so not to be denied,
We played our trump card, the prospect's upside.

In the glare of the upside, technology pales,
And what might be covers for lack of details
The lure of the big one gets AFEs signed,
While visions of science drift slowly behind.

Our strategy worked—the well was approved,
Contracts were let, a rig was moved,
Hole was made, logs were run,
Pipe was set, tests were done.

In one magic moment, as quick as you please,
We struck oil and gas in great quantities
Back in the office we heard, "Nice job, men.
You've served The Board well. Now do it again."

—Don Herron

If Charles Dickens had been an interpreter

DECEMBER 2002

Editor's note: There is a theory that the great satirists are often generations ahead of their time. TLE Editorial Board Member Don Herron recently tested this concept by changing only a few words in a passage from A Christmas Carol. The result is TLE's Christmas card to the SEG membership.

"Forgive me if I am not justified in what I ask," said Scrooge, looking intently at the data, "but I see something strange, and not belonging here. Are they processing artifacts?"

"That might be, for I see them too," was the Team Leader's sorrowful reply. "Look here."

Zooming in on the display, it brought forth two features, wretched, abject, frightful, hideous, miserable. They were pervasive, and clung to the very fabric of the data.

"Oh Man! Look here! Look, look, down here!" exclaimed the Team Leader.

They were two; pale, meager, ragged. Where coherence should have filled the image out, and touched it with much higher resolution, it was as if a stale and shriveled hand had pinched and twisted the data, and pulled events to shreds. No deconvolution, no filters, no signal enhancements, in any grade, through all the mysteries of modern processing systems, could hide monsters half so horrible and dread.

Scrooge started back, appalled. Having them shown to him in this way, he tried to say that he could interpret the data in spite of them, but the words choked themselves, rather than be parties to a lie of such enormous magnitude.

"Team Leader! Whose are these?" Scrooge could say no more.

"They are yours," said the Team Leader, looking down on them. "This one is Multiples. That one is Noise. Beware of them both, and all of their degree, but most of all beware the Multiples, for in them I see that which is written Doom, unless they be effectively removed. Deny it!" cried the Team Leader. "Slander those who tell you of them! Admit it for your factious purposes, and make it worse! And bide the end!"

"Have I no refuge or resource?" cried Scrooge.

"Is there no disk space?" said the Team Leader, turning on him for the last time. "Are there no workstations?" ▶

Characteristics of an interpreter

JANUARY 2003

Over the course of a career spanning almost three decades, I've met interpreters of all shapes, sizes, and temperaments and have had occasion to wonder what are the professional and personal characteristics that make a good interpreter. I think the qualities that best suit an individual to be an interpreter are not necessarily academic, in that there is no direct or obvious correlation between the level of higher education achieved and career success (however one might define this). Rather, the most important qualities seem to be grounded in personality, in the approach and attitude an interpreter brings to the job and also in the profound and intimate sense of satisfaction that motivates one to do this kind of work. You might say these qualities are the "right stuff," an ideal blend of technical ability and innate personal traits that broadens and deepens with maturity and experience.

In this admittedly subjective context, I offer the following list of characteristics of an interpreter. The list is not exhaustive (or exhausting) and certainly is not in any order of importance.

1. You are naturally curious about the earth.
2. You are flexible enough to handle multiple interpretive possibilities for virtually every project you'll ever see.
3. You can tolerate the criticism that you're never working fast enough.
4. You have sufficient self control to hold back tears when thinking about all the good science you could have done with all the data you've seen.
5. You are committed to doing a task that some people think can be done routinely by anyone, and about which most people really don't want to hear any details.
6. You are able to withstand second guessing of your work by people who have limited understanding of the manner in which the work is done.
7. You have sufficient thickness of skin to watch and not comment when your work is presented or used without acknowledgment.
8. You can accept that your professional skills base may not be thought of as a specialty.
9. You can visualize geology in three dimensions without the latest advances in visualization tools and technologies, and you can use those tools as enhancements to, not replacements for, fundamental visualization skills.
10. You have highly developed pattern recognition skills.
11. You are aware that much of the time you'll be working alone, even in the contemporary team-oriented business environment.
12. You recognize that no single workstation system or application package will ever enable you to perform all the interpretive tasks you'll need to do.
13. You have learned that your interpretation skills are complemented by your knowledge of data acquisition and processing.
14. You willingly take responsibility for the output of automated processes whose workings you don't always fully understand.

15. You appreciate that, no matter how good your seismic correlations look, they must always be modified to fit wireline log and biostratigraphic correlations.
16. You know the difference between a model-based interpretation and a model-guided interpretation.
17. You know the difference between accuracy and precision.
18. You understand your own limitations as an interpreter; in the words of C. Hewitt Dix, you know for yourself "when no correlation is possible."
19. As a consequence of characteristic 18, you have the courage to say out loud that you know your limitations as an interpreter.
20. You have learned from experience that there are only two types of interpretation: those that have been revised and those that need to be.
21. You are aware that not many of your interpretation projects will ever be tested by drilling, and, of those that are, some will be after you've transferred to other projects.
22. You have learned to carefully document your work because your maps and reports speak for you long after you've moved on.
23. You realize that no interpretation is complete until its attendant uncertainty has been thoroughly described.
24. You eagerly read *TLE* each month (of course you do). ▶

Chapter 2: 2003

How much data can an interpreter pick

FEBRUARY 2003

Editor's note: It is routinely accepted that applied geophysics is divided into three specialties—data acquisition, data processing, and interpretation. The skills and productivity of the first two areas are relatively easy to describe and benchmark. Those of the latter remain, after three quarters of a century, elusive of quantification and perhaps even of definition—although surveys indicate that about half of SEG's members consider themselves interpreters. This article inaugurates a new series in TLE *whose aim is to close that gap in the professional lexicon. Interpreter Sam is fictitious, but the situations described are extrapolated from real incidents.*

This is the story of Interpreter Sam, the Everyman of the interpretation world. He's the fellow sitting at his workstation in the office or workroom down the hall. You don't necessarily know him very well and may not even know his name, but you know what he does and have something in common with him. You may have heard of his work and are somewhat familiar with his reputation—perhaps once you preceded him on a project, or perhaps he followed you. You've seen him in the lobby or the parking garage and gone a little out of your way to greet him. You might have recognized him from a distance on the exhibition floor at an Annual Meeting and exchanged nods of acknowledgment. In terms of what it means to be an interpreter, you are in many ways the same.

Why do we call him Sam? It's no more or less fitting than any other name, and carries no implications (any similarities to other persons, real or imaginary, are unintentional and purely coincidental). There are famous individuals with the same name—Sam Adams, the venerable Uncle Sam, Yosemite Sam (a crotchety sort like some interpreters I've known), Kauffman Medal winner Sam Allen, Fessenden Award winner Sam Worden, and of course the popular Sam Gamgee. Everyman has a name, and ours is Sam.

On an otherwise average morning we find Sam in his office working on a particularly difficult correlation problem. He is fortunate enough to have an office with a real door, a solid one with oiled metal hinges that he can open or close depending on his mood and the task at hand. At this moment the door is slightly ajar, and all who know Sam understand that this means he doesn't want to be disturbed.

A light rapping followed immediately by the nearly imperceptible swish of the door tells Sam he is no longer alone. He turns to see his coworker T. J. in the doorway. T. J. has recently been promoted to team leader of an exploration group whose primary objective is to conduct the initial evaluation of a new basin in which his company has gained an interest. This is his first foray into supervision, and T. J. is counting on Sam to support him and give him helpful advice, especially when it comes to planning the seismic interpretation that T. J.'s group will do.

"Sam, I need to do an estimate of manpower requirements for my new project. I've got more 3D data than I can get my arms around, and I'm not sure if there are enough geophysicists in my group to interpret all of these data in time. If you could tell me how many miles of seismic data a good geophysicist can interpret

> *He is fortunate enough to have an office with a real door, a solid one with oiled metal hinges that he can open or close depending on his mood and the task at hand.*

per day, then based on the amount of data I have I can estimate whether or not I need more geophysicists to meet my schedule."

"Do you mean your schedule was made before you knew whether or not you had enough people to do the work?"

"Don't worry about that, Sam. Just tell me how many miles of seismic data a good geophysicist can interpret per day."

"I don't think there's a simple answer to that question."

"Why not? You're a senior interpreter, and you've seen a lot of data in your career. You should know how many miles of seismic data a good geophysicist can interpret per day."

"First of all, it's not just a matter of how much data you have. You need to know something about the geology of your basin, how variable your data quality is …"

"Come on, Sam, I'm not asking for a doctoral thesis. I just want to know how many miles of seismic data a good geophysicist can interpret per day."

"Okay, T. J., but you have to consider also how many seismic horizons you'd need to interpret in order to accurately characterize the basin. This isn't always obvious at the outset of the project, and changes as the project progresses. Of course, you know the amount of time needed for interpretation increases as the number of horizons to be interpreted increases . . ."

"Sam, you're overworking the problem here. I'm not asking for a detailed analysis, I only want to know how many miles of seismic data a good geophysicist can interpret per day."

"T. J., if you're going to have more than two or three interpreters working on this project, you need to recognize that no two interpreters go about their work in the same way. Often an interpreter alters his approach to a project when he's working on a team as opposed to when he's working alone. This is neither right nor wrong but is fundamental to interpretive style and certainly affects how a project proceeds. What I mean is that doubling the number of interpreters on a project doesn't mean the work will be done twice as fast, to say nothing about the quality of the work …"

"You're definitely going off topic now, Sam. Why can't you just answer my question? How many miles of seismic data can a good geophysicist interpret per day?"

"It's like I said before, there isn't a simple answer to that question. I'm only trying to explain why . . ."

"Thanks for your time, Sam, you've been very helpful. I have a much better idea now about how I'll plan the interpretation work for my project."

With that T. J. left as quickly as he had come, leaving the door open. But only a few seconds had passed, hardly enough time for Sam to turn back to his workstation, when he heard T. J.'s voice in the hallway. He was speaking with his supervisor.

"I had a conversation with Sam about the manpower estimate for my project, and I've decided how many geophysicists we'll need for the 3D interpretation. I'll get my recommendation to you by the close of business today."

Sam got up from his chair and walked over to the window (he's fortunate enough also to have an office with a window). He needed a break to be sure that he hadn't just spent the last 10 minutes talking to himself. ◗

APRIL 2003

Sam turned the corner and was walking down the hallway toward his office when he saw his department manager striding purposefully toward him. There was sternness in his step, and when his eyes acquired and locked on to his target, Sam realized that their impending encounter would not be by chance. His manager needed something, and he needed it right away.

There would be no perfunctory greeting or polite small talk.

"Sam, I have to present the Block 46 prospect to upper management tomorrow afternoon. As part of my presentation I'll need a slide of a regional map to set the prospect in its regional context. Don't make it too busy or complicated—keep it simple. You know what I mean, show only the major faults. Have it ready tomorrow morning so I can look it over before the presentation."

Sam knew that requests like this never are simply or quickly handled. Based on past experience, Sam thought he probably would have to redo this slide several times before his manager would approve it. Sam figured that this happens because, although a good interpreter, he is a poor mind reader.

Today Sam's problem was more serious than a temporary shortage of clairvoyance. Being most familiar with all of the mapping that had been done for Block 46, he knew that there were no regional maps covering the prospect area. There was a good reason for this. Sam's company is relatively new to the Block 46 area, and no one had gotten around to compiling a regional map from the collection of postage-stamp maps that had been produced following the initial lead sweep through the area.

"I don't think we have a regional map for the Block 46 area."

"No matter. I need a regional map for the area by tomorrow morning."

"Are you saying that I need to draw a regional map for the area by tomorrow?"

"Whatever it takes."

Sam was very well aware that the most talented team of interpreters on the planet could not interpret and map in less than 24 hours an area even half the size of that needed to provide a sensible regional context for Block 46. But he did have an idea of how he could produce a regional map that would suffice. He could

> *" ... the map flashed past the audience like a meteor shower on a moonless West Texas night, there for an instant and then gone."*

reduce his Block 46 prospect map to an appropriate regional scale, and, with the reduced image in the center of his regional template and using his admittedly cursory knowledge of the regional geology of the area, he could literally draw structure contours and faults freehand to fill out the rest of the template. A syncline here, some steep dip there—yes, a normal fault would look good right over here. He would take great care to ensure that the map would be consistent with the two or three display lines used to illustrate the prospect. There would be no grid of control lines or 3D survey outlines on the map; only the locations of the display lines would be shown, so no one was likely to ask to see a line in this or that direction that might compromise the regional structure as "mapped." Remember, the map wasn't supposed to be too busy or complicated, because if it were it might spawn unwanted questions.

Sam went about his work, and by the end of the day had fashioned a regional map that by most standards could be judged both aesthetically pleasing and geologically reasonable. He slept on the matter that night and reviewed the map in the morning before sending it to his manager. It wouldn't be accurate to say that throughout this exercise Sam didn't ask himself what he was doing and why he was doing it. He never heard anything about that day's presentation or whether the regional map was even used. He never saw the map again, but since then he has wondered if it ever found its way into other presentations.

Several months later Sam attended a talk in which one of the first slides shown was a regional map. In the ethereal world of darkened rooms and animated PowerPoint presentations, the map flashed past the audience like a meteor shower on a moonless West Texas night, there for an instant and then gone. Sam almost asked the speaker to back up one slide so he could look more carefully at the regional map, but thought better of it. There was something vaguely familiar about the map, and Sam wished he could have a few words with its author. ❯

Move your pick down, move your pick up

June 2003

For the past few weeks Sam had been working on a regional mapping project. He was interpreting two horizons, one relatively shallow in the prospective section and one much deeper. He had tied both horizons to his only control well several tens of miles away and was having difficulty carrying the deep horizon in some areas owing to the poor signal/noise ratio of his data at depth. He had abandoned thoughts of sensibly interpreting seismic facies in the deep section and now was mapping structure as best he could—form mapping, you'd call it, in simple terms.

On this day Sam was correlating his deep horizon through a particularly troublesome area, one of those where picks diverge into the noise, and how you decide to take your horizon through makes all the difference on the other side. He was concentrating on an extracted line through this area when his supervisor came into his office.

"How's it going, Sam?"

"Pretty good, Dave. I've been working on a line across that especially noisy area in the southeastern part of Region 2, and I've finally found a good correlation through it for my deep horizon. Have a look."

Sam wasn't hesitant to ask Dave's opinion, because Dave had worked as an interpreter for several years before moving into his supervisory position. He pulled up a chair next to Sam and looked closely at the line displayed on Sam's workstation.

"Looks OK to me, Sam, but I wonder if your pick might be a little too high here, about one cycle too high."

Before Sam knew it, Dave grasped the mouse and repicked the deep horizon where he thought it should be, one cycle lower than Sam's pick.

"There, that's much better. Let's see how that fits with the rest of your interpretation. … Oh, look at the time! I'm going to be late for a meeting! I'll check back with you later."

Dave got up and left, and so Sam went ahead to see how Dave's revised pick would affect his interpretation. He hadn't looked at many more lines when he found it necessary to change Dave's pick back to where he had originally placed it. Nevertheless, Sam was pleased to have followed up on Dave's suggested change, because in doing so he gained greater confidence in the interpretation he had done up to that point.

On the very next day, Sam happened to be reviewing his horizon picks on the same extracted line that Dave had changed when Dave's boss, Bob, stopped by his office.

"Dave mentioned that you've been working on a regional mapping project. Can you show me some of your data?"

Bob, who like Dave had some interpretation experience in his background, sat down next to Sam and looked at the extracted line.

> *He couldn't help but laugh a little when thinking about this self-justification of his own interpretation—as experience had taught him, having a good sense of humor is very important for a practicing interpreter.*

"This is an interesting line. You've picked two horizons here? Looks to me like you have a serious problem with signal/noise in the deep section."

"Yes, I've gone over my correlation for the deep horizon on this line several times now."

"Well, it seems to me that your deep horizon is a little too low right there."

Bob pointed to the same spot on the extracted line where only yesterday Dave had said that Sam's pick was too high.

"You should raise your pick about one cycle there."

Not sure whether he was hearing a suggestion or an order, Sam slowly moved the cursor to the line and raised the pick while Bob watched.

"There, that's much better. You're doing a good job, Sam. Keep up the good work."

Now, of course, Sam had to repeat yesterday's effort of checking the effect of the revised pick on the rest of his interpretation. He spent the remainder of the day carefully doing this, and by late afternoon still had not reconciled the change. He was spinning his wheels and decided it would be best to stop for the day and begin fresh the next morning. He had learned that correlation problems such as this one are not solved when you're tired, so he shut down his system and went home.

The following morning Sam spent two or three hours reviewing the changes that Dave and Bob had suggested. He concluded that in order for his final interpretation of the deep horizon to hold together, in light of the poor signal/noise of his data, he would leave the horizon in the problem area exactly where he had originally picked it, one cycle above where Dave had thought it should be and one cycle below where Bob had thought it should be. Sam rationalized this decision by saying to himself that in statistical terms the final position of the horizon was simply the mean of its three possible positions. He couldn't help but laugh a little when thinking about this self-justification of his own interpretation— as experience had taught him, having a good sense of humor is very important for a practicing interpreter.

One week later Sam completed his regional map of the deep horizon, being particularly careful to ensure that the contours accurately reflected his pick in the southeastern part of Region 2. To his knowledge the final pick in the problem area was never again questioned or reviewed. ▶

Memories of mentors

AUGUST 2003

Sam was on his way to visit Janice, one of the company's new hire geophysicists, to see how she was doing on her current interpretation project. Janice had been with the company for slightly less than a year and was one of three geophysicists assigned to her project. As the least experienced member of her team, Janice followed the lead of the other interpreters in what you might call an apprenticeship. Sam, as a senior interpreter not working on Janice's project, was helping her in what his supervisor described as Sam's mentorship role. Sam welcomed opportunities to share his knowledge and expertise with Janice and other less experienced interpreters—it seemed like the natural thing to do. Several years ago the company had instituted a mentorship program that Sam had enthusiastically joined, but he'd always wondered why the company found it necessary to formalize mentorship. He figured that the reasons for doing so didn't really matter, because mentoring occurs in a healthy organization whether part of a formal program or not.

Janice smiled when she saw Sam in the doorway.

"Hi, Sam. I'm so glad you could stop in. There are a few problem areas in my project that I need someone with experience like you to look at. I can't seem to make any good correlations through these areas—I'm stuck."

"Let's have a look. Perhaps I can make a few suggestions to help you get through the tight spots."

Sam knew, of course, that even if he did quickly see solutions to Janice's problems, he couldn't just tell her what to do. Rather, he would need to guide her in the right direction so that she could see on her own what to do. Sam thought this is how mentoring should be done.

After Janice showed Sam a map and a few seismic displays, he asked her to describe her correlation problems as concisely as possible and draw a simple sketch or two to illustrate them (using cross sections or plan views). Then he asked several probing questions about her interpretation strategy and knowledge of the company's workstation software. Before too long Janice began to think of alternative approaches to her problems, and Sam offered some suggestions on what to try first and how to tell whether or not a given approach was useful.

"I'd never thought of that! Now I see another way to correlate my faults and will be able to visualize the correlations much more easily. Thanks!"

"Glad I could help. But don't forget you still have a lot of work to do."

"You seem to be able to see correlations after looking at these data for only a few minutes, when I couldn't see them after looking at the same data for days. How did you learn to do that?"

"Well, I suppose it comes with having seen a lot of data and having made a lot of correlations, some of which were good and some not so good. An interpreter can never see too many data—there's always something to learn from a new data set. You also have to keep up with the latest developments in interpretation technology such as visualization applications. But when you come right down to it, many of my skills probably came from having worked with senior interpreters when I was

> *Memories of time spent with senior geophysicists in those years welled up, and he felt a deep sense of gratitude to those men and women who had selflessly done so much for him.*

a new hire like you. I learned a great deal simply by watching what they did, and every now and then they said something…"

Sam stopped short, because he felt himself launching into a sermon, a tendency that had become more pronounced, and of which he was becoming increasingly aware, as he grew older. He didn't want to start telling war stories—lately he had been doing more than enough of that while loitering in the break area.

"I should be going now, Janice. Let me know how your project goes from here, and call me if I can help."

"Thanks again, Sam."

Sam became wistful as he walked back to his office. His pace slowed as he reminisced about his early years, when he was Janice's age. Memories of time spent with senior geophysicists in those years welled up, and he felt a deep sense of gratitude to those men and women who had selflessly done so much for him.

He remembered one man in particular, Harry, and one specific incident with him. Twenty years ago Harry was the most highly respected interpreter in the company. He had met virtually every interpretive challenge a geophysicist could face in those times. When Harry entered the drafting office, no one needed to be told that his job could move to the front of the line with no questions asked. He had earned his stripes by doing the work and not just talking about it.

Harry had come by Sam's office to help him with one of his first interpretation projects. The project included several 2D data sets varying in quality from poor to unusable and laid out in irregular overlapping grids. This was in the days of paper record sections, when there was only one print of each line available. The whereabouts of field tapes for these data sets were unknown, so reprocessing to improve data quality was out of the question—what you saw was what you interpreted.

Harry spent 15 or 20 minutes with Sam looking through his data and asking questions about the progress of his work. Then he straightened up, thought for a moment, and, with palms flat on Sam's drafting table, leaned forward and looked directly into Sam's eyes.

"You know, Sam, many years ago, before you were born, there were a few people in this company who, after spending several weeks looking at these data, could interpret a few miles of it. But they're all dead now."

To this day, when Sam tells this story to other interpreters, they are speechless, just as he was 20 years ago. ▶

Seeing green that wasn't there before

OCTOBER 2003

Sam and his supervisor, Dave, attended a meeting for review of exploration activity in a frontier basin in which the first round of drilling following a lease sale had just commenced. Sam's company had won the crestal blocks on what was generally regarded by the industry as the top prospect in the sale (the Gamma Prospect) but had not yet spudded a well on it. One of the company's major competitors was drilling the first well in the sale area on its highest bid lease (the Delta Prospect), located several tens of miles to the west of Gamma. As fortune would have it, Sam had mapped Delta, but the company had considered it to have much greater risk than Gamma and so had not bid competitively for it.

Review of the status of the Delta well was one of the first items on the meeting agenda. Dave would speak for the exploration group, and he began with a quick summary of the latest scout report. He described the progress of the Delta well by referring to a seismic line that tied the well and extended eastward across the Gamma structure. While Dave was speaking, Sam noticed that the interpretation on the display line had been changed from when he last saw it no more than a week ago. Previously a single horizon (the "red" horizon) had been interpreted to define the top of the primary prospective reservoir interval in the Gamma-Delta area, but now a second horizon (the "green" horizon) had been added beneath the red horizon. This new horizon was present at Gamma but converged with the red horizon to the west toward Delta, with the effect that the thickness of the prospective red-green interval was zero at the Delta well location.

At this moment Sam listened very carefully to Dave, who now was explaining to the assembled managers and staff that the Delta well most likely would be dry because the primary prospective interval, interpreted to be present on Gamma, was probably absent at Delta. The results of the Delta well to date, as far as they were known, seemed to support this interpretation. Dave's analysis appeared to sit very well with everyone, and, when he finished speaking and returned to his seat, the mood in the room about the upcoming well on Gamma was very positive.

As the meeting continued, Sam leaned over to Dave and asked him a question.

"Dave, I don't remember having seen that interpretation of the green horizon that you just described. When was that done?"

"There are times when you have to tell them what they want to hear."

Sam knew exactly what Dave meant. There was no well control close to either Gamma or Delta, and the depositional and basin history models for the area were far from well constrained. The quality of available seismic data in the area was such that interpretation of the green horizon as Dave had shown it was possible, but not at all obvious or necessarily even likely. The outstanding virtue of the green horizon was that it explained the Delta well results while still casting favorable light on the undrilled Gamma Prospect.

This interpretation supported the original technical decision to risk Delta more highly than Gamma, which had ultimately led to the business decision to bid more aggressively for Gamma rather than Delta. Sam thought that the interpretation of

Chapter 2: 2003 17

> *There are times when you have to tell them what they want to hear.*

the green horizon was speculative, even though it was consistent with the fact that the Delta well had not logged any sands over the depth range corresponding to his best depth estimate for the prospective red-green section in the well. But who could really know—the Delta well was wildcat drilling at its best, and the company would drill the Gamma Prospect no matter what the results of the Delta well. As had happened before and no doubt would happen again, the optimism of exploration tilted uncertainty in its favor in the absence of, or in spite of, data to the contrary.

Before the year was out, Sam, Dave, and many other people would know that both the Delta and Gamma wells were dry. Sam moved on to another group and never heard any explanation for the failure of the Gamma well. ▸

The horde of peons that make maps

DECEMBER 2003

Sam's supervisor was unable to attend a quarterly R&D review and asked Sam to go in his place. Arriving five minutes before the meeting was scheduled to begin, Sam noticed right away that he was the only exploration geophysicist in the room. He introduced himself to the chairman and indicated that he would represent his supervisor from the Exploration Department in the meeting.

The chairman started the meeting on time (a marvel in itself, Sam thought—most of the meetings he had recently attended started at least five or 10 minutes late), briefly went over the agenda items, and then proceeded with the first review topic. According to an agreed format, each speaker on the agenda would give an update of his or her research topic. Each presentation was supposed to be no more than 10 minutes long and would be followed by open discussion of the topic, again to last no more than 10 minutes. As the meeting went on, Sam observed that some topics generated very lively discussions, while others passed by with no comments at all. The meeting concluded on schedule, and Sam remembered thinking what a good job the chairman had done keeping the meeting on track.

As he was getting up to leave, Sam heard two research geophysicists across the room talking.

"I missed the first few minutes of the meeting. Who was that sitting two chairs to your left?"

> *But I can tell you this, within these walls we can do much better than calling each other names.*

"Oh, he's Sam, Sam what's-his-name. I didn't catch his last name. He was sitting in for some supervisor in the Exploration Department. I think he's an interpreter, you know, one from that horde of peons they have that do nothing but make maps…"

Sam wasn't sure whether or not this was said intentionally for him to hear, but either way the words made him uncomfortable. He collected his things and quickly left.

The next day one of Sam's fellow interpreters, Jack, stopped to speak with him in the hallway.

"Sam, I heard that you went to yesterday's R&D review. How'd it go?"

"Not too bad, I suppose. The meeting was run very well, much better than the way ours are handled. They talked about a lot of interesting topics, but honestly, some of what I heard went way over my head. There were times when I wanted to ask a question but didn't. I guess I was afraid I'd sound foolish or stupid."

"I know what you mean. I attended one of those reviews last year and came away with exactly the same feeling."

"I did hear one comment I wish I hadn't. This one guy referred to us as a horde of peons that do nothing but make maps."

"Really? Well, I've been called worse before. You know, once I heard someone call the R&D group a gaggle of geeks who write programs that no one ever uses."

"I hadn't heard that one. We sure can get creative when it comes to making fun of each other, can't we? All kidding aside, though, what do you think of our R&D group? I've heard some pretty nasty criticism of them, and I don't think the people doing the criticizing were kidding."

"I think they do pretty well, considering that they're usually the first to get hit when budgets are cut. I don't know who else could provide us with the technology we need to solve our exploration problems. The contractor community certainly can't do the job all by itself."

"I agree with you. We need both our own R&D and contractors, but in what proportion? How do we strike the right balance between internal R&D and external services?"

"I don't know. But I can tell you this, within these walls we can do much better than calling each other names. We can begin by listening, really listening, to each other more closely and not hesitating to ask questions about each other's work, no matter how stupid we think we'd sound."

By the end of the year Sam's company had undergone another reorganization, part of which included major restructuring of the Research Department. Sam learned the names of the two research geophysicists he had overheard in the R&D review only after he found out from a friend that both of them had been let go as a consequence of the reorganization. ▶

Chapter 3: 2004

A visit from home

FEBRUARY 2004

The previous evening Sam and his wife, Jean, had talked about her bringing their two young daughters (ages 4 and 6) by the office on their way to a doctor's appointment. The children had visited Sam at work several times before and very much enjoyed seeing the place where their father went every day. These visits weren't intended to be programmed events such as "take your child to work" days; rather, they were simply family activities but without a hidden purpose (no Mary Poppins engineering an outing to the Fidelity Fiduciary Bank here).

Sam went down to the reception area to meet his family, and then escorted them to his office. Once there the girls seated themselves in front of Sam's workstation, the younger on his lap, and eagerly asked him to make pretty pictures appear on the screens. They were captivated by the bright colors and animation, and were especially delighted when Sam rotated or zoomed in and out on the displayed images.

"Daddy, what are those colored lines there?"

"Those are what we call wellbores. They are tracks of the holes we drill into the ground to find oil and gas."

"That one looks like a straw sticking out of a milk shake."

Sam showed them a display of a seismic line, and, as he picked a horizon across the line, described how he was tracing layers of rock deep below the surface of the earth. The girls understood very little of what Sam was saying, and didn't ask him any more questions—not that they weren't curious, but because they were so absorbed in all the color and movement. Sam thought it better that they don't ask, not now. The time will come when they'll ask more than enough questions, most of them about matters much more important to them than why Daddy is doing this or that in the office.

The visit lasted about 45 minutes, and for Sam the time passed all too quickly. Jean gathered the girls up amid their mild protests and guided them out of Sam's office. They weren't four or five doors down the hall when their attention had already turned to what kind of trinkets the nurse in the doctor's office would give them after their appointments. As he waved goodbye, Sam thought about how much they meant to him, and wished he could walk away from his work and focus his attention elsewhere as easily as his young daughters seemed to be able to do.

After lunch Sam attended a meeting that began well but finished poorly, with not much of interest in between. One of the attendees was of the type who, for various good reasons, is very difficult to listen to, even for only a few minutes. As often happens, this individual dominated the meeting; he alone spoke for the better part of an hour, frequently interrupted other speakers, and carried on loud side conversations, being completely unaware of his effect on everyone else in the room. He was impervious to questions except those he wanted to answer, and those only because he could turn them to support his point of view or gave him an opening to expound on one of his pet topics. As the meeting wore on, Sam sensed the good feelings built on the foundation of his family's visit slowly slipping away, but, mercifully, the meeting ended before they had dissipated entirely.

> **❝ Daddy, is your work just coloring pictures and listening to other people talk? ❞**

At home that evening Sam came through the door with more smile than frown on his face. During supper he told his family how much he enjoyed their visit, and asked his daughters what they had liked the most.

"I liked watching you draw colored lines on the TV! Why can't we do that on our TV?"

"Maybe some day we'll be able to do that, but not on our old TV, that's for sure."

Sam and Jean exchanged a glance, being careful to show neither amusement nor worry. Jean then asked Sam about the rest of his day, and he described how the afternoon meeting with the tiresome speaker had seemed to go on interminably. When he had finished, his older daughter spoke up.

"Daddy, is your work just coloring pictures and listening to other people talk?"

Sam looked into her earnest face and marveled at the innocence and simplicity of her question.

"Well, yes, I suppose it is." ▶

Finding the perfect match

April 2004

Sam was walking through the exhibition hall at the SEG Annual Meeting when he saw coming toward him two of his oldest friends in the business, Ken and Tom. Sam, Ken, and Tom had first met as new hires at Gargantua Oil, where they worked together for about three years and got to know each other quite well. They had passed those years and become friends by way of common experience and dissolution of preconceived notions and misplaced expectations. Each had subsequently moved on to another company, either through the hope of improving his chances for building a career or finding more challenging work—in the best of all possible worlds, those two goals would coincide for them.

Engrossed in their own conversation, they hadn't noticed him yet, so Sam quickened his pace to be sure to catch their attention before they turned down another aisle. He was only a few steps away when Ken looked ahead and saw him approaching. He nudged Tom, and both men came up to Sam with genuine smiles on their faces.

"How are you, Sam? How long has it been since we saw each other? Wasn't it a few years back at the Annual Meeting in Houston?"

> *All three men shared a heartfelt laugh ... the unpretentious kind that only good and old friends can share.*

"I think it was, Ken. Yes, I'm sure it was, as sure as an aging interpreter can be. You know, at my age and in my position on the demographics curve, I can't depend on my memory to be all that accurate anymore."

"We know what you mean. Tom and I were just kidding about the same thing. It seems as though there's so much going on these days and so many names, faces, places, and passwords to remember, that we can't keep track of it all anymore, even with the latest in digital personal planning technology."

"So that's what you call it, digital personal planning technology?"

"It's as good a name as any, although there probably are more formal names. I'm old school, I suppose, still writing notes to myself and sticking them in my pocket or tacking them to the wall. I was doing that even before we had Post-it Notes—remember when those first came out?"

"Ken, only a few minutes ago I was telling you about the quality of my memory, and you're asking me to remember that far back? You mean you can't recall what I just said to you about that? You're as bad as I am, if not worse!"

"Take my word for it, he's much worse."

All three men shared a heartfelt laugh with this exchange, the unpretentious kind that only good and old friends can share.

"So how are you two enjoying the meeting?"

"Pretty well. Attendance looks to be up, and many of the exhibitors think we're about to go on an upswing. Of course, that could be wishful thinking, or perhaps I'm a victim of some very effective sales pitches."

"How many technical sessions have you been to?"

"Only a few. I have a tough time with more than two or three talks in a row, you know, in a darkened room and rarely with enough time for any good questions, much less any good answers to either good or bad questions."

"I feel the same way. As a matter of fact, Tom and I bumped into each other as we were leaving one of the technical sessions and decided to come to the hall to see if we'd run into any old friends. And here you are!"

"I'll take good luck and coincidence any day, if that's what this is."

"Are you fellows hungry? It's getting on toward lunchtime, and we might not be able to find a place to eat if we wait much longer."

"Sounds good to me. Did you want to find a local restaurant, or should we just get something here in the hall?"

"Let's stay here, that would be easiest. Maybe we can have dinner together tonight at a really nice place."

"Only if you're buying."

They made their way to one of the snack bars outside the hall and bought sandwiches and sodas for lunch—they needed nothing fancy, because the main course would be conversation.

"So, Ken, you've been with Behemoth Oil for, what, seven years now? What's that been like?"

"It's been what I expected, up and down, and fortunately more up than down. I went through the usual honeymoon phase for the first six months or so, and then I found out what the company was really like. There's plenty of room for good work to be done and some decent folks to work with. Can't really ask for much more."

"What's their stance on technology? Does your management support you, and I mean not only when times are good and the oil price is high?"

"There are times when I think they know exactly what I need and others when you'd think we're not speaking the same language. One thing they don't do is interfere with my actual interpretation work. It's really very simple—they give me a data set and tell me to interpret it the Behemoth way."

"If that's the only problem you have, then you're the luckiest man in the oil patch. At my company, they give you an interpretation project and enough time to do a decent job—you know, not enough time to overdo it, and just enough time to do better than a half-way job. Then, when you think you're done, they review your work and tell you to interpret the data set the company way."

At this point, with tongues nearly bursting through the cheeks of all three men, Tom spoke up.

"Let me tell you what happens at Colossus Oil. I've worked there for six years now, and it wasn't until last year that I finally figured out what's expected of me as an interpreter. For the longest time I'd thought there was a specific Colossus way to interpret seismic data, but I was wrong. They don't give me a data set to interpret like you guys get. Instead, I get a completed interpretation, and I have to go find a data set that fits it." ▶

JUNE 2004

There aren't many quiet times in Sam's normal work week, but, when they do occur, most often they are right after lunch (assuming he hasn't worked through lunch). On this day, right after lunch, Sam was gazing out his office window, focusing on nothing in particular to give his eyes a break from the morning's work. His mind was wandering through halls of memories with no special place to go and soon found a resting place in thinking about a former coworker named Fred Henning. Sam was an aspiring young geophysicist with the company when he first met Fred. In those days, Sam gave very little thought to his surroundings other than to how they could assist his upward career movement—you know, work a few years, master all there is to know about geophysics in the oil and gas business, and step up into management as soon as possible. One thing he had thought he couldn't let happen was to become another Fred Henning.

> **"Who in his right mind would want to spend each and every day for years picking seismic sections and making maps?"**

No doubt there is one Fred Henning, maybe several, at every oil company (the majors, at least). He was the stereotypical fellow who long before you met him had moved or been moved off the management track, who now spent his days doing nothing other than interpreting seismic data and making maps. The Fred that Sam knew was about 50 years old (Sam wasn't really sure, because he never asked his age, or much of anything else, for that matter—he didn't want to get too close to someone like Fred). He occupied a small but meticulously kept office. The contents of this office were the unpretentious basics of the time: desk, desk chair, drafting table, map rack (nearly full of rolled paper and film maps), guest chair, a file cabinet or two, and a bookshelf. Remarkable only in hindsight, the bookshelf in Fred's office held very few books or manuals of any kind. Sam had thought, how could this guy know anything? He has hardly any books or course notes—no wonder all he does is sit there and make maps! He had a framed picture of his wife and family on his desk, but Sam never bothered to ask about them.

What Sam remembered most about Fred was the consistent approach he brought to his work. If he passed by Fred's office in the morning and happened to glance in, usually he saw a neat stack of prefolded seismic prints on one corner of his desk, next to which was an array of finely sharpened Colerase pencils. Somewhere close by was an engineer's scale, a map weight or two, an electric eraser, and not much else. Later in the day if he passed by Fred's office again, Sam saw the same scene, with one difference—the stack of prefolded sections was now on the opposite corner of his desk, with another horizon or two completely interpreted on the sections. Sam recalled that Fred's sections were annotated in minute detail, a characteristic Sam has seen unmistakably in the other senior interpreters he's known. He remembered also that Fred's maps were simply beautiful, elegantly contoured and with no need for drafting, the kind of maps you can't create from a machine no matter how hard you try.

Sam finds himself thinking about Fred Henning much more now than he ever did even just a few years ago—as a matter of fact, he most often thinks and talks about him in a broader sense, because, after having followed his own career path, he's realized how much in the man he didn't see. He had viewed him only in the context of their jobs, and, even at that, only as he had perceived the importance of those jobs from his own point of view, still relatively immature to the real workings of business and life. At one time he had thought of Fred as some sort of failure, a management washout, or a burned-out technocrat, a dinosaur set in old ways and soon to be extinct, who was still around only because the company couldn't or wouldn't do what now is so easily done in the name of change and improved business efficiency. The young bucks could look at him and say to themselves, "Why do you keep him around? We can work as fast as he can, and look how much potential we have for advancement! You can get just as much, if not more, from us as from him, and at much less cost to the company!"

There was more to Fred Henning than what Sam had taken the time to find out. He had assumed that you couldn't ever choose to pursue a career in the manner that Fred had. Who in his right mind would want to spend each and every day for years picking seismic sections and making maps? Decades ago Sam couldn't imagine how someone could opt for such a career. Looking back, Sam knew that there were more than a few good reasons why a man like Fred was where he was, and that he had been remiss in not getting to know him better, and in not asking, without being presumptuous, what his own views of his life and work were. When and why did he make his career decisions? What were the critical junctures for him, and not just in his work? Sam never asked Fred about the picture on his desk, or to hear war stories about his good old days, nor did he try to get him to talk about his own hopes and dreams. What Sam did get from him were straight answers, an honest, soft-spoken "I don't know" if he honestly didn't know, and a subtle smile when he made a good play at the lunchtime bridge game.

Sam guesses that Fred is retired now, and, if still living, he is enjoying his well-earned retirement with those unnamed people in the picture on his desk. His time in the business was not marked by numerous publications, honorary degrees, or society medals, but rather by several hundred or a thousand maps or more, most of which were forgotten or lost very soon after he finished them. This probably is the same contribution the majority of interpreters will make in their careers, and Sam is sure Fred had those few maps that once made a substantial or even crucial difference in some past successful venture, just like all interpreters hope to have. Of course the real measure of Fred Henning is the one Sam failed to fully appreciate in the time he knew him, that of the experience he brought to bear on his work, that he readily would have shared if only Sam had made the effort to ask—experience not only in things technical, but also in character, in embodying the ideal that in doing your work consistently well, no matter what that work is, you are a success.

Sam is at a stage in his life and professional career when he often feels very much like the Fred Henning he knew must have felt. As he stepped out of his reverie and turned to his workstation, Sam took consolation in the thought that he could do much worse than to be another Fred Henning. ▶

Measuring success

AUGUST 2004

Sam had been assigned to a project on which he would be responsible for both acquisition and processing of the data he would subsequently interpret. He hadn't often worked on a project like this; most of the time he wasn't deeply involved in data processing and picked up details of the processing flow from another geophysicist or read them in a contractor's report (if such a document even existed or hadn't been misplaced). In these instances he knew even less about the acquisition of his data, and, if asked any questions about it, only parroted what he had gleaned from available reports.

Sam was not so detached in this project. He actually had played a significant role in designing his survey (a relatively tight grid of 2D lines) and selecting acquisition parameters, and he had worked closely with the contractor throughout the data processing. Now he was prepared to interpret a data set whose strengths and limitations he knew better than anyone else. He was the only interpreter on the project, and the buck stopped with him—he would be working without a net.

The interpretation itself held its challenges. The faulting in the project area wasn't overly complex, but Sam did have to be particularly careful with the faults at depth where they soled out into a deep layer of salt. There were stratigraphic features to be mapped, especially in the main target interval, and Sam recognized early in the project that integration of this aspect of his work into the whole interpretation would be critical in risking his prospect. He had two nearby wells for control, and, because of his earlier involvement in processing, he knew the phase of his data and could make his well ties with confidence.

Sam interpreted a total of eight horizons, concentrating mostly on his main target section and the intervals immediately above and below. He was working on a horizon below the base of the target interval when his supervisor came into his office.

"Sam, you've been working pretty hard on your interpretation for the past few weeks now. When do you expect to be finished?"

"I have this deep horizon to complete, and then I'll start on the well proposal."

"Yes, we'll need that soon. The partners have been making a lot of noise lately about getting this prospect drilled as soon as possible."

"When do you think we'll be able to have a meeting with them to see what their interpretation looks like?"

"I don't know. Let's just take care of our business first, and then we'll worry about their interpretation. Hopefully theirs won't be very different from ours."

By the way Sam had arranged his office, with his back to the door while sitting at his workstation, it was possible for someone to quietly enter the room without his noticing, especially if he was looking at another person seated in the guest chair opposite the door. Sam realized this could happen but regarded it as a shortcoming he could live with in having his own office, as opposed to working in an open office environment. Now, while he had been speaking with his supervisor, the exploration manager had come into his office and was listening

> *For an instant, Sam wondered if his supervisor was asking a trick question. What is success? Does he mean technical success, commercial success, a victory over partners regardless of well results, or is there some other definition of success he has in mind?*

to their conversation. Sam's supervisor had seen him enter but made no move to acknowledge his presence. Caught up in the discussion of his work, Sam was not aware that the exploration manager was standing right behind him and continued to address his supervisor.

"OK. It would be a shame to do all this work and then not be able to drill the prospect. I realize I'm biased, but I sure do like this one—it's one of the best in our inventory and has been a great project for me."

"So you've enjoyed the technical challenges in this project and don't mind working alone?"

"I don't mind at all."

"If we do end up drilling this prospect, what would have to happen for you to consider your work a success?"

For an instant, Sam wondered if his supervisor was asking a trick question. What is success? Does he mean technical success, commercial success, a victory over partners regardless of well results, or is there some other definition of success he has in mind? Sam answered reflexively and honestly.

"The well would be a success if formation tops came in within my predicted depth ranges, the primary target reservoir was good quality sand, and that reservoir was charged with moveable oil."

At this point, the exploration manager spoke for the first and only time.

"No, that is not your measure of success. Your measure of success is getting the well drilled."

With that the conversation was over, and the exploration manager and Sam's supervisor left his office.

About two years later, Sam heard that the prospect in fact had been drilled, and, although both his depth and lithologic predictions had been very accurate, the well unfortunately was dry. Sam was disappointed and wondered what else he might have done to better understand the charge model for the prospect. More than anything else he remembered the lesson he'd learned about success being in the mind of the beholder. ▶

Remembering Dad's advice

OCTOBER 2004

Sam accompanied his supervisor, Dave, to a meeting called by one of the teams in the company's International Exploration Division. Dave knew that several years ago Sam had worked on a short-term interpretation project within the limits of the new venture area that was to be discussed at the meeting, and he thought that Sam might provide some technical backup in case certain questions about the geology and geophysics of the area came up. Without being explicitly told so, Sam thought from the outset that this was the primary, if not sole, purpose for his attending the meeting. He had been to meetings like this before as a relatively junior staff member where, remembering his father's favorite sayings about small children in large groups, he would be expected to "speak only when spoken to" and "be seen and not heard."

On the way to the meeting, Dave asked Sam about the interpretation he had done in the area.

"Dave, it really wasn't all that much of an interpretation. We had a very coarse grid of 2D time-migrated lines, so coarse that we could map only regional trends. Our only well control was almost 100 miles away and gave us very little information other than the gross lithologies of our mapped intervals. Believe it or not, we actually did come up with some broad estimates of recoverable reserves for the area, but the error bars on the estimates were huge. We really didn't have any good feel for net/gross or porosities or recovery factors but went ahead and made some ballpark calculations anyway."

"Well, there are times when that's all you can do, given the information you have."

"I sure hope no one has ever used those reserves figures for planning purposes, because I know we could do a whole lot better with more data."

"That's always the case."

When they arrived at the meeting, Sam quickly saw that he was the only person there who was not at least a team leader. He was becoming uncomfortable because he sensed that this meeting would be conducted at a much higher level of business than he had expected, and he was sure he'd be out of place. His fears were a bit allayed by the cordial greetings he received, but his uneasiness persisted. He promised himself that he would speak only when spoken to.

The meeting began well, as some but not all do. The chairman called the meeting to order at the scheduled starting time, electing not to penalize those present by making them wait for those who were not on time. As he briefly reviewed the agenda, it became clear to Sam that although there were many items to be discussed, there really was only one objective for the meeting—to find a way to complete an interpretation of the new venture area as soon as possible.

To the casual observer this objective would not have been apparent. The first few points of discussion revolved around whether or not a new 3D survey would need to be acquired, which contractors would be asked to bid for the job, who would provide acquisition QC, how much onboard processing would be needed,

> *The chairman called the meeting to order at the scheduled starting time, electing not to penalize those present by making them wait for those who were not on time.*

would the processing be done in-house or by the acquisition contractor or by a different contractor, and so on. It seemed as though each one of the attendees had his or her own opinion or experience that was at odds with everyone else's opinion or experience. The discussion at times degenerated into three or four individuals speaking at once, and it was only through the concerted effort of the chairman that anything remotely approaching consensus on data acquisition and processing was reached, and at that the collective wisdom decided only that another meeting several weeks hence would probably be needed. At this point the chairman mercifully called for a break. Sam noticed that a healthy number of attendees wasted no time in availing themselves of the facilities.

The next part of the meeting concentrated on interpretation of the new venture area, centering on review of existing regional studies and development of a work plan for detailed interpretation of the area. The regional review was concise and effective, and then the discussion of the work plan began. To Sam's surprise this discussion proceeded very smoothly and with very much less contention than before—it seemed as though all present knew exactly what had to be done. But to his dismay Sam learned that the "what" of the interpretation was the easy part, and the "by whom" was much more problematic. Conversation became very frank, about which interpreter of which reputation might be available, or which supervisor could spare whom for how long. Sam was now very uncomfortable because many of the people being discussed were acquaintances of his, and he thought he might be hearing things he wasn't supposed to hear. Soon his discomfort gave way to irritation because the discussion was going nowhere. To him, any of these people could probably do the job, so why didn't they just draw up a list of candidates and ask directly whether any of them might be interested? This seemed too simple—and then, before he knew it, Sam went against his own good sense and spoke up.

"I worked on a small project in the new venture area several years ago and recall that there had been plans to acquire a spec 3D survey over the area. I think that survey actually was shot and processed and probably is available for purchase. A friend of mine at Massive Oil has seen a few lines from the survey and told me that the data quality is very good. If we bought that survey, it probably wouldn't be difficult for me to incorporate and then extend my existing interpretation across the entire area. I'd have to look at the data myself before I could estimate how long the full interpretation would take…"

"Sam, that's an excellent idea! I'm certain we have money in the budget to purchase that survey. You call the contractor and set up a meeting to view the data. Dave, I'm sure it won't be any problem for you if Sam works on this project for a while. Does anyone else have any comments? No? Well then, that concludes the business of the meeting. I've made our arrangements for lunch, so we'll adjourn now and meet at The Club at 11:30."

The conference room emptied faster than it had at the break, and Sam found himself alone with his thoughts. After a few minutes more, he found himself alone in his office eating the lunch his wife had packed for him. He mused about the two lessons he thought he had learned before but obviously had not—that there are times when one should speak only when spoken to, and that interpretation is more easily discussed than done. ◗

Examining staff's handiwork

December 2004

Sam was returning to his office when he noticed another interpreter in his group, Steve, gazing intently at a map hanging on the wall outside of their conference room. Sam couldn't remember having seen a map there when passing by that room earlier in the day, so, being curious, he walked up and stood beside Steve to have a look at the map for himself.

"You don't see many maps like this anymore, Sam. I can hardly believe it—a hand-contoured, hand-drafted, and air-brushed structure map! This is a real throwback if I ever saw one."

"You're right. I can't think of anyone who doesn't use computer gridding and contouring for his maps these days. I didn't even know we could still do these here. Who's the author?"

"Let's see—it says 'Staff' in the title block. I've seen that before. We usually use that name when we don't want anybody to know who really worked on the map."

"Well, I guess it doesn't matter who did it. It certainly is an attractive map, especially with the air-brushed colors. It takes a lot of time to create maps like this, but they look really good."

"Sam, I heard it said once that for structure mapping, there isn't a computer gridding and contouring package on the market that can beat hand contouring when it comes to representing details of complex structure. I remember one of our guys in the potential fields group saying that he felt comfortable with computer contouring only when using it on gravity or magnetic data because it's most effective on regularly spaced data that don't involve interpretation of any kind. He thought it was very useful for identifying bad points in his data sets, which show up as bull's-eyes that can be very quickly edited."

"I suppose that's right, Steve, but you know how it is now. Almost everyone uses computer contouring, to the point that there probably are a lot of younger people whose only experience with hand contouring came while they were still in college. There just isn't much demand for that skill anymore."

> *As he continued to scan the map, he saw that more and more contours were out of place. The map began to unravel before his eyes.*

While Sam was speaking, his eye was drawn to a particular feature in one of the more structurally complicated areas on the map. This feature appeared to be what Sam had heard described as a "knife-edge" contour—that is, a single contour bounded on both sides by contours having the same value, in this case deeper than the single contour. He visualized a cross section through the feature, and saw it as a "tepee-like" structure with the apex corresponding to the location of the "knife-edge" contour.

"Look here, Steve, it's a 'knife-edge' contour. I'm surprised to see this. Usually people just ignore a single-point high like this or simply draw a small closed contour to honor the highest point of the structure."

"I see it too. You know, computer contouring wouldn't do something like that."

Sam didn't really hear Steve, because now his eye had moved along the fault that bounded the "knife-edge" contour to the north and found another feature that was much more problematic.

"Have a look at the contours along this fault. Do you see anything wrong?"

Steve took a closer look and noticed that the contours as drawn indicated that the throw diminished and actually reversed along the strike of the fault and then went back to the original sense of displacement before the fault tipped out. As he continued to scan the map, he saw that more and more contours were out of place. The map began to unravel before his eyes.

"Sam, unless this fault is interpreted to be a strike-slip fault, which I don't think it is, there's a serious contouring error here. Worse, look what happens as you follow these contours here away from the fault. We'll need to get back to the people who made this map and look at their trace data to see what the actual interpretation is. That's something I'm not too comfortable doing."

"I know what you mean. It's too bad we can't tell from the map itself what the input grid of interpreted lines is. If we knew that, we might have some idea of how to pinpoint the problem lines and determine how extensive the problem really is. You know, that's another difficulty we face more often than we'd like—having to look at maps on which there is no representation of the control used to make the map in the first place."

"You know, Sam, I was just wondering, what if this map had been computer contoured? If that 'knife-edge' contour had been handled differently, we might not have looked more closely and found these other problems."

"You and I both know that there's no excuse for not checking a map for structural validity, whether contoured by computer or by hand."

"That's a lesson I'm sorry to say I've had to learn more than once."

"There's another lesson here, one that we'll have to pass on to the authors of this map. When it comes to interpretation and mapping, there are only two types of maps: those that have been revised and those that need to be." ▶

Chapter 4: 2005

JANUARY 2005

This morning Sam was going to the office of one of the geophysical service contractors that his company regularly used for specialty data processing. His visit would be only part business; he intended to spend some time catching up with a good friend of his, Jim, who worked for this particular contractor. Sam hadn't called ahead to let Jim know that he was coming—he would drop in unannounced, as he had done many times before, in the style of folks in a small New England town who visit each other at all times of the day and who are always welcome to sit at the kitchen table or on the front porch (weather permitting) and share stories over fresh coffee and a piece of homemade pie.

Sam signed in at the receptionist's desk and then sat down to wait for Jim to come down and meet him. When he saw Jim approaching, Sam noticed that there was a certain resignation in his step and a slight droop in his shoulders, both of which were uncharacteristic of Jim's usual manner. Sam wondered if there might be something wrong.

"Good morning, Sam. It's always good to see you. How are you today?"

"Very well, thanks. How about you? Quite honestly, as you were walking up I thought you looked like something was bothering you."

"As a matter of fact, there is. Do you remember that over the past few months there had been quite a few rumors about our company being bought?"

"Yes, I do recall hearing some of those but didn't pay much attention. You know what they say, talk is cheap."

"Well, those rumors have become fact. As of this past Monday, we're now wholly owned by Bigger Fish Geophysical Services."

"Really? I didn't think that would ever happen. What does this mean for you?"

"I don't know yet, but we've been assured that our day-to-day operations will continue unchanged, at least for the time being."

"Knowing you the way I do, Jim, I suspect you've already taken the opportunity to express your feelings about this in your own unique way."

"Of course I have! And here is what I have to say."

Jim handed Sam a single sheet of paper, on which the following verses were written:

A SHORT (?) HISTORY OF GXT

About one score less five years ago
In our leaders, a thought started to grow.
Parts of our business we don't like.
Perhaps we should tell them to take a hike.

Modeling, processing, and interpretation were too slow
But a database with seismic data was the way to go.
They had tried seismic gathering, but it didn't pay
However many many dollars did fly away.

> *Knowing you the way I do, Jim, I suspect you've already taken the opportunity to express your feelings about this in your own unique way.*

So out into the cold cruel world we were thrown
With very little of anything we could call our own.
Things were real shaky for quite some time
We were making our way with hardly a dime.

But as often happens in a nursery tale
Up rode a white knight before we did fail
He supplied us with funds that were sorely needed
But even with this our progress was not unimpeded.
The modeling area had really slowed
And how to improve it no one knowed.
The processing we had was too small to carry the day
Some other path seemed to be the only way.

We heard of a French company called a dataid
They had lost funding and of going broke were afraid.
Somehow some way a deal was put together
And it was figured out that we might be birds of a feather.

Originally we thought that selling the system would ease the pain
But it became apparent that selling the service would make the gain.
Depth imaging for hire became our battle cry
And it became the path that we would abide by.

We changed our way of thinking and the things we do
We added time processing many data problems to subdue.
Many people were added our programs to improve
And many many more to produce services in the groove.

We did not forget a very important need
Lack of data in house our progress would impede.
So several peddlers we convinced to come and work with us
Through the years they have paid for their seats up on the bus.

Imagers, developers, processors, and sales
Working together needed help with the details.
Our management handled most of these with ease
And the bean counters really showed their expertise.

Now it has come to the news we heard the other day
A suitor with much money has come along our way.
They like our style and the growth that we have achieved
And that continued good work can really be believed.

We had to do something and this is very true
The white knights wanted their money back as was their due.
Additional capital was needed if we were to survive
With more funding we can stay together and thrive

It seems that we can stay together and continue to move along
With a new big brother to help keep us strong.
Our fearless leaders have really done us proud
Our thanks to them should really be expressed out loud.

Ending up with a company with all our various strengths
With what they had to start with is going many lengths.
Rest assured that we must be aware that changes will occur
But after the recent years if this bothers you—WHAT FER.

Sam smiled broadly as he finished reading.

"Jim, you've said it all. Two or three years ago, who could have imagined this? Better yet, what do you think your company will look like two or three years from now?"

"Who knows? We'll see."

(Many thanks to Jim Patch, the resident poet at GXT and a member of SEG since 1952.) ▶

Finrus and the Block 289 farm-out

FEBRUARY 2005

One of Sam's first tasks for the exploration team into which he'd recently transferred was to help prepare for a review of the Exploration Department's prospect inventory. Being new to the team, he regarded this as an excellent way to quickly familiarize himself with the inventory. He was charged with putting together a one-page summary of each of the prospects that had been assigned to him; this summary would include a structure map for the primary target level, a single display seismic line illustrating important geologic elements of the prospect, and critical economic and risk/uncertainty information.

While collecting material for one of his prospects, the Block 289 prospect, Sam noticed on the display line what appeared to be a flat spot about 1000 ms above the main target section. This anomaly was somewhat subtle but could be seen with reasonable confidence to cut across several dipping reflectors and terminate against a fault. Sam didn't have a map at the level of the anomaly to check for structural conformance and also didn't have any other seismic lines on which the anomaly might have been visible. He looked through the existing documentation

> *We just don't have time for details like this.*

for Block 289 but found no mention of or reference to a flat spot at any level on the prospect. He thought it would be best to tell the inventory coordinator, Marie, about what he had observed, and so he took the display line to her.

"Marie, I've been working on the summary sheet for the Block 289 prospect. I think I see what might be a flat spot on the structure in the section above the main target interval. Has anyone ever seen a feature like this before?"

"No, not that I know of. Is this what you mean? It does look interesting. When you get some time you should probably look into it a little more. For now, we need to finish the inventory summary as soon as we can. We just don't have time for details like this."

"Don't you think we should at least amend the summary to reflect the possibility of a flat spot? If it is a bona fide direct hydrocarbon indicator, it certainly would improve the risk we're currently carrying for Block 289."

"As far as I know, we're not concerned with prospectivity in that interval. We and our partners are more interested in the deep potential on this block. We really don't need to bother with it now."

After the inventory review was completed, Sam had the opportunity to do some careful interpretation on Block 289. In addition to reviewing the interpretation of the deep prospective level on the block, he also took the time to interpret two new horizons, an upper horizon at the level of the flat spot and a lower horizon approximately 200 ms deeper. He observed that the flat spot could be consistently correlated from line to line and that its areal extent coincided closely with the limit of structural closure he had mapped for his upper horizon.

Sam was very encouraged by these results but was equally disappointed when he presented his interpretation at the next partners' meeting for Block 289. Everyone listened politely as he spoke but, for reasons he didn't understand, both his own management and the partners dismissed his work, preferring to concentrate exclusively on the deep potential on the block. This situation was made all the worse by the fact that the companies couldn't agree on a drilling location within the block to test this elusive deep potential. The meeting ended, as Sam learned later, as most meetings on Block 289 had ended before—with pledges to do more technical work to define the deep potential but no real progress toward making a decision to drill a well.

Good fortune prevailed, and several weeks later Sam moved on to begin interpreting a new 3D survey over another of his prospects. He soon forgot about Block 289 and didn't attend any more partners' meetings for the block (he assumed that if there had been any meetings, he hadn't been invited). About six months passed, and Sam never heard about any plans to drill a well on Block 289.

And then one day Sam heard that the company had farmed out its interest in Block 289 to a small operator, Farm-Ins 'R' Us (colloquially known as Finrus). It turned out that Finrus held several exploration leases to the north and east of Block 289 and also had interests in several producing fields nearby. Sam did a little research into this production and learned that one of the producing intervals could be correlated to the level at which he had observed the flat spot in Block 289. Now being more curious, Sam found out that Finrus had taken the farm-in without reviewing his company's data package for the block. To top it off, Sam's company had kept only a minimal override in the deal.

Not a week passed before Sam read in the weekly scouting report that Finrus had spudded a well in Block 289. Immediately Sam spotted the well location on his map at the level of the flat spot and saw that the well was near the center of the area of the anomaly. Within a month Finrus announced that it had made a gas discovery on Block 289, and Sam noticed that the TD of the well was almost 3000 ft above the estimated depth to the deep target that had commanded so much of his company's attention. Finrus drilled three appraisal wells in quick succession, and then announced plans to install a production facility on its new field. They had a commercially attractive development in the midst of established infrastructure, and the deep potential on the block remained untested.

There are times when Sam blames himself for having not made his case more strongly for the flat spot on Block 289, and he wonders if the allure of the deep potential on the block was merely a distraction rather than a viable exploration play. There are other times when Sam is feeling cynical, and he thinks that what really happened with Block 289 was that his company simply couldn't find common ground with partners and decided it was easier to farm out the block. ▶

Verifying preconceived notions

APRIL 2005

Sam and his good friend Jack were assigned to interpret and map an area for which their company was preparing to apply for an exploration license. This work had been farmed out to Sam's group because the overseas office under whose jurisdiction the area of interest fell was understaffed and wouldn't be able to finish an interpretation in time to meet the host country's licensing schedule. At the same time, another interpreter in Sam's office was starting a regional interpretation of the greater license area, with the intention of providing geological background and context for the technical part of the company's license application. Sam thought it odd that both regional and detailed mapping should be done simultaneously, but he was in no position to question the work plan—it had been set in motion by management in the overseas office, and that was that.

In terms of the interpretation to be done, the project was a very good one. Sam and Jack would be working with an excellent quality time-migrated data set (depth migration wasn't really necessary for the area), which was much better than the irregular grid of mixed vintage data sets their colleague had for the

> *Sam and Jack carefully prepared all of their latest maps and seismic displays for Harvey to review and were understandably eager to showcase their work when he finally arrived.*

regional interpretation. Preliminary inspection of their data revealed that a nearby producing basin would be a very good structural and stratigraphic analog for the area of interest, and so they began the interpretation with great enthusiasm in hope of finding good leads that could be matured into high-quality prospects.

Sam's company had only recently developed a new technique for generating seismic inversions, and Sam and Jack were anxious to try this technology and perhaps use it to highgrade their leads. Unfortunately, there was no well control in their area of interest, and they could only resort to using well data from the analog basin to calibrate their inversions. As a consequence, they assigned much greater uncertainty to their interpretation of the inverted data but still felt that those data strengthened the case for the prospectivity of their leads.

Every other week Sam and Jack sent a note to the lead geophysicist in the overseas office advising him of the progress of their work. After almost three months, and well into their interpretation, Sam and Jack were told that the lead geophysicist, Harvey, would be coming to Houston on business and might have some time to visit with them and review their project. They were quite happy to learn this because they were proud of their work, especially their interpretation of the inverted data, and thought that the area of interest could turn out to be a very good opportunity for the company.

Sam and Jack carefully prepared all of their latest maps and seismic displays for Harvey to review and were understandably eager to showcase their work when he finally arrived. As they began their presentation (nothing as formal as that—it was actually more of what is popularly known as a working session), Sam noticed that Harvey didn't seem to pay much attention to what he was seeing. Sam wasn't sure why this might be, and he attributed it to the possibility that Harvey was preoccupied with one of the other business matters that had brought him to Houston. Although Harvey might not be very interested in their mapping results, surely he would be impressed with the inverted data and their use in establishing stratigraphic correlation to the analog basin. But when they finally showed the inverted data, Harvey reacted quite unexpectedly.

"What did you say this display is again?"

"This is a seismic inversion of the line we're using to make our stratigraphic correlation to the analog basin. These are the results of a new process recently developed by the Technology Group."

"I'm sorry, I just don't see it. What are you trying to do with this? Why don't you simply compare the seismic facies you see on the conventional displays and make your case from that?"

"We've already done that, but we think the inverted data provide additional support for our interpretation."

"Well, I'm not at all convinced of that. As a matter of fact, I'm not too sure I agree with your correlation to that particular basin as an analog."

Sam and Jack were taken aback by this remark. At no time up to this point had Harvey indicated that he disagreed with anything they had said, and now it appeared that he was prepared to dismiss all of it. Being unsure of how to proceed, Sam weakly attempted to continue with the presentation as he and Jack had originally planned it, but Harvey stopped him. In retrospect, Sam remembers being very glad that his and Jack's supervisor wasn't present when this happened.

"What I'd really like you two to do is verify my preconceived notions for this area."

If taken aback before, now Sam and Jack were completely at a loss for words. They waited for Harvey to tell them exactly what his preconceived notions were, but he didn't. Instead, he described some velocity displays he would like to see from the special data processing that was under way for the area, thanked Sam and Jack for their time, and left.

Having not been told to change any of what they were doing, Sam and Jack decided to carry on with their work exactly as they had intended before Harvey's visit. And so they did, and their completed interpretation made up a substantial portion of the license application that the company eventually submitted. As fortune would have it, the company was not awarded an exploration license, and the area of interest that Sam and Jack interpreted is now part of a larger producing province. Well results have confirmed that the structure and stratigraphy of the area are very similar to the analog basin as Sam and Jack originally thought—and as for Harvey's preconceived notions, who knows? ▶

The best meeting ever

JUNE 2005

Sam left home late that morning, and, as a consequence, had to endure unexpectedly heavy traffic on his way to the office. Arriving almost an hour later than usual, he made several circuits through the parking garage before he found a place on the level just below the roof into which he could squeeze his car. In a way, Sam was glad he was late because at this time of day he was spared having to compete with other employees for one of the choice parking spaces on the lower floors of the garage. Property management had recently restriped the garage, and this measure purportedly had alleviated the daily congestion and overflowing of the garage; however, like most short-term solutions to long-term problems, this had only substituted one problem for another. Sam had noticed that the new parking spaces were so narrow that any vehicle larger than a Toyota Camry could barely fit between the lines—needless to say, this challenged the pilots of SUVs

Chapter 4: 2005　　41

> *As he left his office, he wondered why he had been invited to this meeting because he hadn't been able to tell from the vaguely worded e-mail what its purpose was.*

and pickup trucks to attempt extraordinary feats of skill in maneuvering these much larger vehicles into the ever-shrinking spaces.

It was Wednesday, and Sam had spent the earlier part of the week and both of the last two weeks working hard on a very complicated interpretation. On this morning, he was actually quite anxious to get started with his work because he had gone home the previous evening feeling that he was very close to solving the most critical correlation problem in his project. As he powered up his workstation, he thought he had better check his e-mail, just in case there might be some correspondence that required immediate attention. He logged on to his account and found about a dozen new messages, only one of which was marked urgent. He opened that message and discovered that he had been invited to a meeting scheduled to begin in less than five minutes. He looked at his watch and saw that if he hurried, he could just make it. As he left his office, he wondered why he had been invited to this meeting because he hadn't been able to tell from the vaguely worded e-mail what its purpose was.

When Sam arrived at the conference room, he entered as inconspicuously as possible—but, stealth having never been one of Sam's more highly developed skills, he was quickly spotted and his identity immediately questioned.

"Are you sure you're in the right room?"

"Yes, I think so. I received an e-mail this morning inviting me to a meeting scheduled to start at 9 a.m. in room 868."

"Well, this is room 868, so you're in the right room. What did you say your name is?"

"I'm Sam ————."

"Who? I know we invited Sam ———— to this meeting, but I don't recognize you. Although I myself haven't personally met him, I don't think you're Sam ————."

When you've lived your entire life going by the name that your mother and father gave you at birth, it can be disconcerting to find out as an adult that you're not who you've always thought you were. It can be especially upsetting to learn this in a business meeting at a company for whom you've worked for more than 10 years.

Sam showed his ID badge to the chairman of the meeting, who frowned at it and harrumphed.

"Yes, you're Sam ———— all right, but not the Sam ———— who should be in this meeting. What do you do, and who do you work for?"

"I'm a geophysicist, a seismic interpreter, and I work for Dave ———— in the Exploration Department."

"Oh, that's the problem. You're Sam ———— the geophysicist, but we invited Sam ————, the engineer, to this meeting. My assistant must have accidentally selected your name from the address book instead of his. Yes, your names are probably right next to each other on the list. Sorry about that. We really do appreciate your taking the time to come by, but we won't be needing you today."

Sam left the room as quietly as he had entered. Reassured that he was still Sam ———— the geophysicist, he walked back to his office feeling both satisfied and amused. He considered that meeting to be the best he'd ever attended. ❱

John's checking my ties

AUGUST 2005

Sam had been with the company for about two years before he was assigned a project on which he would essentially be working alone. Previously he had always worked with a senior geophysicist, who as project leader would set their objectives, priorities, and schedule; obtain resources; go to meetings; and generally keep middle management at bay so they could keep to their schedule. This time Sam would do these things for himself, knowing all the while that there would be several sets of watchful eyes and helping hands in the wings to keep him from going too far afield or floundering badly. After all, the company did want the project to be completed, and so much the better for all concerned if both the project and Sam were successful.

Sam's project involved regional interpretation and prospect generation in a small basin affectionately known as the Shale Basin, so named because the only well ever drilled in it had penetrated almost 15,000 ft of monotonous shale section and encountered virtually no reservoir quality rock of any kind. His most pressing technical challenges were that he had no experience interpreting and mapping in the structural style of this basin, and his seismic data consisted exclusively of a loose grid of six-fold, 2D time-migrated lines. If these weren't enough, the lone well in the basin had only a partial suite of wireline logs to use for identifying mapping horizons. In one of those strange interpretive relationships in which what appears at first to be a serious problem turns out to be a blessing, Sam very quickly learned that his single control well actually afforded him considerable freedom in carrying his correlations away from that well—lack of well control had opened space for interpretive creativity (within the bounds of reasonable geology, of course). Sam plunged into the project with great enthusiasm, and before long he had produced his first structure map, of which he was justifiably proud.

Sam had hung his first map on the wall in the conference room and was carefully checking his contouring when two senior geologists, Larry and Bill, entered the room.

"Is this your first map for the Shale Basin project?"

"Yes it is. Do you think it looks okay?"

"Well, to be sure I'd need to look at a few of your interpreted lines to see whether or not you've honored your data, but on the surface (ha ha) it looks pretty good."

> *I think you've done some nice work here, especially in terms of the quality of data you have.*

"Why did you contour your map with blue pencil? We usually contour all of our structure maps with standard #2 lead pencils."

"Come on, Bill, give him a break. It doesn't matter what color the contours are, as long as they're geometrically correct and don't violate his data. You have to admit, though, it looks like the kid can contour."

"I still don't like it."

Bill then left the room, but Larry stayed behind for a minute.

"Don't worry about him—he's just set in his ways and doesn't easily warm up to anything different from what he's used to. I think you've done some nice work here, especially in terms of the quality of data you have. Keep it up."

"Thanks, Larry, I really appreciate that."

Later that week, Sam received a phone call from John, one of the company's most senior geophysicists and a very highly respected interpreter. In his assurance role, John often reviewed interpretations in progress to offer criticism and suggestions (although not in a line position, he did wield considerable influence when it came to making technical recommendations to upper management). John made an appointment to meet with Sam in the following week, at which time Sam would bring all of his sections and maps to John's office to review his project. Sam had heard some hall talk about these reviews, and, although he had been told that they were "normal" and only a "formality," his anxiety grew from the moment he hung up the phone to the instant before he knocked on John's office door, sections and maps in hand.

"Come in, Sam, I've been expecting you. How are you this morning?"

"Honestly, I'm a little nervous."

"You have nothing to be nervous about. I conduct reviews like this all the time. May I please see one of your structure maps?"

"I've only finished this one."

"That will be fine, we'll start with it then. Contouring in color, I see—haven't seen that for a while. Your contouring looks very good, smooth and uncomplicated. While I look at the map, would you please arrange your dip sections for me in sequence from west to east?"

Sam did as he was asked, and after John had finished with the map, he began to unfold the dip sections, laying out several of them in sequence, one above the other. Then he asked Sam for the northernmost strike line, which he folded at its intersection with the first dip line. He slid the strike line back and forth along the dip line around the intersection point, said something to himself that Sam didn't quite hear, and then repeated this procedure several more times for other dip and strike lines. After a few minutes of this he turned to Sam, who had been watching him intently.

"I'm not checking your ties here, Sam."

Sam nodded and said nothing but thought to himself, if you're not checking my ties, then what are you doing?

John resumed his methodical review of Sam's sections. He didn't look at all of them, perhaps only one-third or fewer, but to Sam it seemed like he looked at each and every section at least three or four times. The review lasted less than 30 minutes, but Sam felt like he had aged five years in that short time. When John was through, he refolded all of Sam's sections and, smiling ever so slightly, handed them back to him.

"Your work is very good, Sam, thorough and consistent. Thanks for coming by."

And with that the review was over. Sam returned to his office, somewhat in a daze from the experience of his first solo project review. Oh well, he thought, if my key still works in the door tomorrow, I guess I'll know that I passed.

Many years and interpretations later, Sam thinks about John's review of his project much differently than he did in the weeks immediately after the actual event (incidentally, several more wells have been drilled in the Shale Basin, the results of which have allowed the basin to unfailingly live up to its name). When he was younger, Sam had thought that John's line-by-line examination of his work was motivated solely by the company's lack of trust in his interpretive skills. Sam still believes that there was an element of this in the review, but he now understands that John's deeper purpose was to gain familiarity with Sam's project not by evaluating only his maps but by looking carefully at the data from which the maps were made, thereby enabling him to form a true assessment of the quality of the interpretation. Sam has concluded this after having been on both sides of the table in project reviews too numerous to count, during many of which superficial assessments of quality and accuracy of interpretation were made after looking only at finished maps, often without seeing any seismic data other than a display line that had been carefully chosen to show only what the presenters wanted others to see. He wonders why there seems to be less interest in looking at seismic data these days, and in his own way wishes that John were still around to check his ties. ▶

October 2005

Sam had made his escape to the coffee bar for his customary mid-morning break. He'd learned to step away from his workstation for five or ten minutes at this time, if at all possible, to rest his eyes and disentangle the tortuous threads of thought that the day's interpretation effort had so far spun in his mind. This respite had become habit to him because he'd found himself concentrating on his work most intently in the early hours, when he was most prone to overexert himself and diminish his ability to work effectively for the remainder of the day. Of course, there were times when he could substitute going to a meeting for taking his break.

> *I made a judgment about which application to use and felt like I was being told after the fact that I was wrong to have made that choice.*

The upside of this was that the average meeting can provide a good opportunity for resting (he had long ago recognized this, being a veteran meeting attendee), but there also was the accompanying downside that the meeting might be more debilitating than having gone on working without a break.

This morning there was no meeting for him to attend, so he sat alone in the break area, drinking a cup of the industrial-grade coffee provided free of charge to employees and visitors alike (the outstanding characteristic of the beverage was its price, certainly not its taste). On some days Sam would return to his office to finish his coffee and gaze out his window, imagining faraway places he'd like to visit and trying not to notice the snarl of traffic on the freeway below, but today he was blissfully soaking in the ambience of the windowless coffee bar, which had been built out on a plan he'd once heard described as "retro airport lounge." Although the contemporary style of the area was not particularly inviting and almost forbidding in its sterile furnishings (you might feel truly guilty if you spilled something or didn't push your chair all the way in before you left), Sam considered it much improved over the previous décor, which always had reminded him of the waiting room in his dentist's office minus the plastic plants and year-old dog-eared magazines.

Sam was about to return to his office when a fellow interpreter, Jim, entered the break area. His face bore a hybrid expression of perplexity and bewilderment, and Sam needed no words to tell him that Jim's day was not going well.

"Jim, you look like you've been doing one of the things on your list of the top three things never to do. What's the matter?"

"I just got out of what I thought was supposed to be a prospect review. It started out to be that but sure didn't end up that way."

"What happened?"

"You're familiar with this prospect I've been working on for the past few months, aren't you? Last week my supervisor thought we should review it with a small group of people, mostly other team leaders, to make sure that we're doing the right things and not doing anything we really don't need to do. We were also going to begin thinking about how we would risk the prospect."

"Sounds like the normal course we run."

"We weren't ten minutes along when one of the team leaders asked which application I'd used to do my interpretation. I answered that I'd used our standard system, SeisWise, and then he asked why I hadn't used WhizPick, you know, that new package we just bought."

"Yes, I've heard about WhizPick and seen a few demos, but I haven't used it myself yet. Like most applications, I've heard both good and bad things about it."

"Well, it turned out that I opened Pandora's box on this one, because the team leader thought I should have used WhizPick because it's more efficient. I began to explain why I'd used SeisWise for my interpretation, but then a couple of the other team leaders started to argue about the virtues and vices of different interpretation systems and which is better or faster or more efficient or cheaper or just about any other adjective you can think of to describe how we work. This went on for the better part of an hour, and it was as though the prospect didn't matter anymore—almost as if the results of my work weren't as important as the manner in which they were obtained."

"Jim, that reminds me of something I read in one of Stephen Jay Gould's books, words to the effect of judging work by its quality and not by whether it was done with what he called maximally fashionable machinery. Of course he was writing in the context of academic research, but I think his idea applies to us as well."

"I suppose so, Sam, but Gould wasn't in the room to bail me out. The review even turned to whether there weren't more analyses I could have done if I hadn't spent so much time with my correlations using SeisWise, and if I had used WhizPick then I'd have had the time to do that work. How could I respond to that? I made a judgment about which application to use and felt like I was being told after the fact that I was wrong to have made that choice."

"What happened to your prospect?"

"That's the best part. No one in the room ever questioned whether my interpretation was consistent or had been fully integrated with all of the other available data. We never got around to that. We spent so much time haggling about the interpretation software that we had to adjourn because everyone had other meetings to go to—everyone except me, that is."

"So you ended up here with me. Why don't you grab a cup of coffee? I can stick around for a few more minutes and probably can stand another cup myself."

Jim found a clean mug and filled it with what little coffee was left in the pot.

"Sam, I haven't been around for as long as you have, so I have to ask you, have you ever been in a situation where you spent a lot of time working on a project, and then someone looked at it for a few minutes and told you that you could or should have done it another way?"

"Yes I have and more than once or twice. But I've learned to accept that kind of criticism because many times it's well intended, and for the times when it isn't, it's not worth thinking about. Besides, no matter what you do or how you do it, there always will be people who will think you're not interpreting fast enough." ▶

If the structure were there, it would have been found long ago

DECEMBER 2005

For several months Sam had been working on a regional mapping project for one of the company's district offices. Assignments to projects of this particular kind were not uncommon because the districts often were heavily involved in well operations or lease evaluations and had neither the staff nor the time to conduct regional studies. Although Sam understood that operational matters must necessarily command highest priority, he always wondered why regional work seemed to slide so easily to the back burner. Like many of his friends and acquaintances in the geosciences, he viewed regional work as a fundamental plank of a successful exploration program. He thought it deserved earnest effort and consistent support and should not be relegated to a hit-and-miss activity mirroring the high and low energy periods inherent in the oil and gas business.

Sam was mapping a part of his project area that contained several producing fields when he thought he saw a very interesting feature in his data, one of those that you always have one eye open for, and, when first seen, never fails to remind you of why you got into this business in the first place. With some detailed interpretation and thorough integration of well control, he mused, this lead could mature into a bona fide prospect and be a positive addition to the district's inventory. The double-edged sword of the feature, its proximity to established production, meant that it would be more attractive commercially and could be risked more favorably but at the same time also could be snapped up by another company at any moment. Sam was understandably enthusiastic, and he took it upon himself to write a technical memorandum, complete with drawings to illustrate the basic elements of the lead (for so he thought it to be), and sent it to the district office.

Several weeks after Sam had sent the memorandum, his supervisor Dave came into his office with a somewhat perplexed look on his face. Sam had learned to interpret many of Dave's facial expressions as precursors to news but not necessarily good news. The one he wore on this day signified not bad but definitely awkward news.

"Sam, several weeks ago did you send a technical memo to the district office in East Barndoor?"

Dave's question caused Sam to feel like the star witness in a high-profile criminal trial.

"Yes, I did."

Give only short answers and don't volunteer any information, Sam thought, until you find out what this is really about.

"In that memo, did you describe a potential lead that you had identified in western Smith County?"

"Yes. Have I done something wrong here, Dave?"

"No, not really, but I wish you had come to me before sending that memo."

> *Sam had learned to interpret many of Dave's facial expressions as precursors to news but not necessarily good news.*

"Why?"

"Well, although I'm sure you meant well, the feedback from the district is that they think you're minding their business. It came to me in words of one syllable that they'd like you to keep to your regional work as they originally requested and leave the prospecting to them."

"Dave, you know I was only trying to help—I wasn't trying to tell them how to do their jobs. But what kind of an explorationist would I be if I saw something interesting and didn't say anything about it?"

"I understand you, Sam, but don't expect everyone else to. Here, have a look at this memo from East Barndoor."

Sam was surprised to see that the memo was handwritten and not addressed to Dave but actually was an internal district memo from one of their geologists to the District Exploration Manager. Sam began to read the memo but stopped when he came to the following memorable sentence:

> [Senior District Geologist] George also stated that people had been looking at the area ever since the first discovery several decades ago, and if a structure as we were looking for existed, it would have been found long ago.

Sam finished reading the memo and handed it back to Dave.

"Well, this certainly hasn't turned out the way I expected."

"Don't worry about it, Sam. You did what any responsible explorationist would have done. But you've learned something—you should know your audience before you begin to speak."

Sam never heard whether or not the feature he saw in Smith County ever came to the attention of any other companies who might have considered it to be drillable. He also wondered how many fields had been found in George's wake. ❱

Chapter 5: 2006

One map for us, another for the partners

FEBRUARY 2006

Sam had worked with a team of geoscientists charged with evaluating a frontier area in preparation for an upcoming lease sale. Most of their effort was devoted to prospect identification and mapping, which was especially challenging owing to the generally poor quality of available seismic coverage in the area. As unsatisfying as it was, their task essentially was "bump hunting," that is, making or breaking prospects primarily on trap geometry, with little emphasis on reservoir presence and effectiveness and petroleum system analysis. Sam had worked on projects like this before and remembered being sorry at the conclusion of each of them for not having been able to integrate more geology into the prospect evaluations—after all, the purpose of interpretation is to describe geology, all aspects of geology, not just structure.

The company successfully acquired acreage on several of the prospects that the team had identified. One of these, designated the Block 68 structure, drew considerable attention because it could be mapped very confidently as a large four-way dip closure, with the added simplification and benefit of being unfaulted (at least at seismic scale, and in view of the poor data quality). The lease blocks on the crest of this feature attracted highly competitive bids, and Sam was pleased when he learned that his company had been awarded Block 68, which contained the crest of the structure as Sam had mapped it. At the same time he noted that a group of three of the company's main competitors had been awarded Block 67 immediately to the west of Block 68. Sam knew that this situation could affect the manner in which the company would move forward on Block 68 because his final map showed very little difference in elevation between Blocks 67 and 68; in fact, the culmination in Block 68 was marked by only a single closed contour above the highest contour in Block 67. If that one contour were removed from his map, which was a real possibility in view of the poor seismic data quality over the structure, then there would be no measurable difference in elevation between the two blocks—and who could tell how depth conversion might alter the structure. Sam had recognized this uncertainty during his interpretation and conveyed his concern to the sale team leader. On his final map he had placed the highest closing contour in Block 68 as his most likely case, and the company had developed its bid strategy based on that representation of the structure.

The company wasted no time in preparing to drill a well on Block 68 as soon after the sale as possible. One of the first activities in which Sam became involved was preparing for a technical meeting with the leaseholders of Block 67, at which the company intended to propose sharing the cost of an exploration well on the Block 68 structure (or was it the combined Blocks 67-68 structure, or even the Block 67 structure?). Sam was a little anxious about this meeting because he didn't know if the Block 67 group might not have done some advanced technical work (e.g., sequence stratigraphic interpretation, burial history analysis, etc.) as part of their evaluation, and so might have good reason for drilling the first exploration well in Block 67—for right or wrong, he wasn't at all apprehensive about any differences there might be between their structural interpretation and his.

Chapter 5: 2006

> *He didn't get past the first display, a structure map he had made for the horizon interpreted to be the top of the primary prospective interval, when he noticed something that he couldn't remember having seen before.*

On the morning of the scheduled meeting, Sam went to the appointed conference room about three-quarters of an hour ahead of time to help set up displays and receive any last-minute coaching that might be given by his management. To his surprise he found his supervisor, Dave, and several other members of the sale team already there, and he saw the walls covered with numerous maps, seismic lines and geologic cross sections illustrating the Block 68 prospect. He greeted Dave and the others and began to review the various displays, especially those about which he might be asked to speak. He didn't get past the first display, a structure map he had made for the horizon interpreted to be the top of the primary prospective interval, when he noticed something that he couldn't remember having seen before. On this map Sam clearly saw that the closing contour marking the crest of the structure had migrated westward and was now located astride the boundary between Blocks 67 and 68. This was not a matter of Recent tilting (postsale tilting, having occurred in the last month or two), continental drift or rectification of some catastrophic cartographic or clerical error that had been found and corrected since Sam last saw the map—no, this appeared to have been done intentionally.

Sam immediately went to Dave and asked him what had happened.

"Dave, my map now shows that the crest of the Block 68 structure is straddling the boundary between Blocks 67 and 68. I don't remember having mapped it that way. What happened?"

"Well, Sam, we decided that we might have an easier time convincing the Block 67 leaseholders to share the cost of an exploration well if we showed them it's possible that the crest of the structure is partly in their block. You as well as anyone know it could be that way, given the data quality over the structure."

"I suppose so, Dave, but couldn't we just say that even though our most likely interpretation places the crest of the structure in Block 68, our seismic data quality is poor enough that the crest could be in their block? That would be a much more accurate statement of our real uncertainty, and besides, given the size of the structure and what little we know about the prospective reservoir section and the charge history of the area, I'd think that a well just about anywhere in Block 68 or 67 could be a valid test of the structure."

"Yes, that could be so, but we've decided to go ahead with the approach I've just described."

Sam wondered who "we" were.

"I think we should present our work as we originally did it and see how they respond."

"I appreciate your concern, Sam, but don't worry about it. You just make your best interpretation, and we'll take it from there."

In spite of Dave's assurance, Sam did and still does worry about it. ◗

Sam visits the 2005 Annual Meeting

MARCH 2006

Sam attended the Annual Meeting in Houston and came away with many impressions, some more lasting than others. As he entered the exhibition hall for the Icebreaker on Sunday evening, he readily sensed the good times that have characterized the geophysical industry of late—these were evident in the glitter of the contractors' exhibits both large and small and in the buzz of conversation that could be heard from every direction. Although not necessarily more spacious than any other facility that had housed previous meetings, the ground floor of the George R. Brown Convention Center seemed to be endlessly vast—even the largest of the exhibits fit into its allocated space with room to spare, and the aisles, although bustling with Icebreaker attendees, seemed wider than Sam remembered from years before. He attributed his awe (if it could be called that) not only to the generally upbeat state of geophysical affairs but also to his own pride in being part of this prosperity in his own small way. After a few minutes Sam walked farther into the hall and had taken only a few steps when he bumped into the first of what would be dozens of colleagues with whom he would renew acquaintance and share experiences throughout the week. This is one of the reasons I attend this meeting, he thought. Perhaps in its own way this is the most important reason, because he had learned that the personal relationships built up over decades were as essential to him and to his profession's health as any of the technology in which he was now immersed.

Amidst all of the wonderful sights and sounds Sam did notice that there might have been something missing—although business was humming along, he didn't see the glamour and glitz that might have accompanied these times; rather, he felt what could only be called a sense of caution or watchful waiting, as though all were mindful that the cyclical nature of the business could manifest itself again, without warning, that US$60 per barrel wouldn't last forever, and that this time they'd see the downturn coming and be ready for it. But this feeling was sufficiently muted (low amplitude, if you will) so as to be easily put aside when Sam encountered more old friends or was drawn to yet another contractor's display. As he strolled up and down the aisles he noticed that the pavilions of the larger vendors didn't dominate his view as they had at other meetings. The exhibition layout seemed to be more balanced, so that he wasn't overwhelmed by certain displays simply because of their location, and as a result he found himself looking more closely at smaller exhibits, in a manner not unlike searching for handcrafted treasures in out-of-the-way booths at the local county fair.

On Tuesday morning Sam repeated a mistake that he had made several times on Monday—he tried to enter the exhibition hall through one of the doors that apparently were for use by exhibitors only (or at least those fortunate enough to be wearing an exhibitor's ribbon). He contemplated fabricating his own exhibitor's ribbon out of whatever burgundy-colored material he could find but thought better of this and resolved to establish a landmark or two that he could use to successfully identify the correct entrance. This seemed to work—he was turned away only once

> *"...he had learned that the personal relationships built up over decades were as essential to him and to his profession's health as any of the technology in which he was now immersed."*

more during the rest of the week. He never did understand why oral presentations began at 8:30 in the morning (with speakers' breakfasts much earlier at 7 a.m.), but the exhibition hall wasn't opened to nonexhibitors until 9 a.m.

At previous meetings Sam, like most other delegates, had picked up many of the small giveaways that exhibitors offered—koozies, note pads, pens, luggage tags, lapel pins (this year some of these were adorned with flashing lights) and many other practical and inexpensive items. This year his sole collectible, other than the water bottle that came in his convention bag, was a green plastic stapler, courtesy of the SEG Continuing Education Program, which he'll use until it runs out of staples (unfortunately this handy little device came with no extra staples, and he hasn't been able to find replacements among his office supplies). If there were any frisbees or other aerodynamic toys this year, he missed them. He noticed also that among all the free things he saw, there was only one not emblazoned with an advertisement or endorsement, and that was the cheese on the cheeseburger you could order in the café on the third floor of the convention center. It might have been that the cheese really wasn't free, but Sam concluded it was after having paid as much for his plain hamburger as the gentleman in line ahead of him had paid for his cheeseburger.

Speaking of convention bags, this year's model continued the trend in basic black of the last several meetings, although Sam prefers the larger bag he brought home from Denver last year. Of all the bags he still has, Sam's favorite is the forest green soft-sider given out at the 1997 Annual Meeting in Dallas. He still carries this bag back and forth to work and wonders if SEG ever will have another as durable and functional as this one.

But Sam's most intense personal experience occurred when he least expected it, and that was early on Monday morning as he walked across the skybridge from the third floor of the Hilton Americas Hotel to the convention center. He happened to look down onto the street in front of the convention center where several buses had stopped to unload delegates. In an instant he remembered a similar sight he had seen on the evening news months before, only that time the passengers on the buses had been hurricane evacuees from Louisiana. He recalled the Saturday on the first weekend after Hurricane Katrina, when he and his wife had spent a full day in volunteer service at the Reliant Arena south of downtown Houston. He remembered the slouching postures and expressionless faces of exhausted, homeless people, suspended in a situation for which even in the deepest recesses of his mind he could find no words to describe. He recalled his conversation with an older man, a retired artist, who had left his home and virtually all of his possessions to the rising water and spent two days on a freeway overpass in New Orleans before making his way to Houston. In spite of all the adversity he had faced, this man had been calm and gracious in thanking volunteers for everything they were doing for him—and then Sam was transported back to the day's reality of the skybridge, the upcoming technical sessions, luncheons and committee meetings, and the parties to come in celebration of the 75th anniversary of SEG.

He walked on to the convention center, rode the escalator down to the ground floor and entered the exhibition hall. On this morning he didn't see the same shapes and colors he had seen the night before, because he was enveloped in a dimensionless image of the same hall filled with evacuees in all states of hope, anger, and despair. How quickly affairs can change, he thought, and how fragile are our circumstances, no matter what our profession. He thought of the retired artist and silently wished him well. ▶

Demurkifying data

APRIL 2006

Sam was on his way to a meeting in which the results of some reprocessing tests were going to be reviewed. As an experienced interpreter familiar with both the data set being reprocessed and the contractor doing the actual work, he had been asked to sit in and comment on the effectiveness of the processing techniques being applied. If the results were favorable, he would help also to identify other projects for which similar processing might be done. As he walked down the hall toward the conference room, he remembered a lesson he had learned several years ago, captured in what is commonly (if not somewhat awkwardly) quoted as Sheridan's rule:

> In comparing two versions of processing of a seismic line, the more recent version having had additional processing applied, if within ten seconds you can't see any significant differences between them, then the additional processing wasn't needed.

Sam entered the room and saw that the meeting had already begun. He recognized all of the geoscientists sitting around the conference table, especially Chris, the geophysicist whose data were the subject of the meeting, and Jack, his good friend and coworker. He was familiar in name only with the others, one of whom looked to be quite bored with the proceedings, and another who seemed very unsettled, as though he had just learned that a large number of insufferable in-laws would be visiting for the upcoming holiday weekend. As he took a seat, Sam saw two seismic images projected side by side on the screen at the front of the room, and he heard Chris discussing the reprocessing parameters for the data. At first glance, Sam could see no appreciable difference between the two displays and immediately thought of Sheridan's rule—but before he could say anything, Jack spoke up.

"You know, Chris, I've been looking at these displays for the last ten minutes, and for the life of me I can't see any real differences between them."

> *I asked you to come to this meeting because I thought you'd contribute some constructive suggestions about my reprocessing project. Instead, you're being flippant and wasting our time...*

"As much as I hate to say it, I think you're right. We've asked the contractor to throw everything he has at this, and we still can't seem to beat the noise problem. I don't know what else there is we can try."

"This isn't the first time I've seen data like these, where the noise is so much a part of the data—almost like the grain is part of the wood of this table. What we really need is to find someone who has a process that can demurkify data like these."

"What did you say, Jack?"

"I said that the noise is as much a part of these data as the grain is part of the wood of this table...."

"No, you used a word I've never heard before. What was it, demurkify, or something like that?"

"Oh, yes, demurkify. You know what that means, to make less murky, to make clearer, to part the fog, to make visible what no man has seen before...."

"Come on, Jack, you made that up. There's no such word as demurkify, and you know it. If you have a serious suggestion to make about the reprocessing, let's hear it."

"I am serious. Who says I can't use that word, even if I made it up myself? We do that all the time, creating and destroying words and meanings to suit our whims. Let's see—we solidify things to make them solid, purify things to make them pure, clarify things to make them clear, and simplify things to make them simple, and then we deplane aircraft, devalue currency, defrost refrigerators, and debottleneck processes, and everyone knows what we're talking about. You know what I meant by demurkify, even if you'd never heard the word before, because it sounded enough like murky to effectively convey my meaning. I think I'm entitled to create words of my own choice and meaning, and, who knows, demurkify might be the one that will become wildly popular and make me famous. Then I won't have to pick seismic for a living anymore."

By this time everyone in the room except Chris could hardly contain his laughter. But Chris was not about to let Jack off easily.

"I asked you to come to this meeting because I thought you'd contribute some constructive suggestions about my reprocessing project. Instead, you're being flippant and wasting our time, and I don't appreciate it, not at all."

At this point Sam could feel the edge in Chris's voice and thought he should intervene before either Chris or Jack said something he would later regret.

"Look, Chris, Jack was just trying to interject a little humor into the meeting. I'm sure he didn't mean any harm or disrespect to you—right, Jack? In any case, you did agree with his assessment that the reprocessing results don't appear to have made much difference. And in spite of how silly he may have sounded, I think we all understood what he meant by demurkify."

"Don't tell me you buy into that verbal nonsense, Sam."

"When it comes to verbs and nonsense, our business may be without peer. And speaking in those terms, based on the last few minutes of conversation here, I think it's time to demeeting and get back to work." ◗

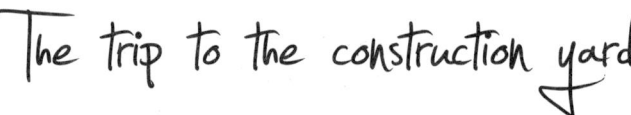

The trip to the construction yard

JUNE 2006

Sam left home on Friday afternoon to drive down to the coast with his family for the weekend. His older children were scheduled to participate in a regional high school athletic event on Saturday and, while they were in the preliminary rounds of competition, Sam, his wife, and younger children were going to visit a construction yard in a neighboring city where a production facility for one of the company's most recent successes was being fabricated. He had called the yard earlier in the week and spoken with the project supervisor to ask if he might tour the facility, and she had very pleasantly agreed to his request, even offering to take him around herself. Apparently it was not a common occurrence for geoscientists to come to the construction yard, and she was glad to accommodate people like Sam who showed interest in the project.

Sam and his family arrived at the yard early on Saturday morning after having dropped off the older children at the natatorium where their meet was being held. He figured that they must have been at least a mile, maybe two, away from the yard when he first caught site of the facility. As they drew closer, the structure loomed larger and larger, made all the more impressive by its contrast with the flatness of the surrounding coastal plain. On entering the main gate, Sam felt dwarfed by the structure, which even lying on its side (it was being built in this configuration) towered over all of the nearby warehouses and office buildings. He knew that this facility would be installed in water depth slightly greater than 1000 ft, so it had to extend at least more than three football fields in length as he now viewed it in its prone position. Sam thought about how simple it is to say that structures such as this are so many feet tall or weigh so many thousand tons, but he marveled at how much more stupendous they are when you actually stand next to one and try to take it all in from top to bottom. He remembered how one of the engineers who had seen the facility at an earlier stage of construction had told him that you could drive your car into any one of the legs of the structure with plenty of room to spare.

Anne, the project manager, cordially greeted Sam and his family at the company's office in the yard and escorted them to a waiting area (not quite a lounge, but at least a space in which you could make yourself comfortable and the younger children had a little room to run around). She told him, as he had expected, that the

> *I've never met anyone who does what you do. I want to thank you because if you hadn't done your job, I might not have my job here.*

children would not be allowed into the construction area, and his wife agreed to stay with them in the office while Anne and Sam toured the facility. After listening to a concise safety briefing and picking up hard hats and safety glasses, they left the office and walked a short distance across the yard to the structure.

As they walked, Anne reviewed the history of the project for Sam. He listened politely and was fascinated by her point of view, which necessarily derived from her particular job in the chain of activity that leads from exploration to production. She briefly recapped the exploration history of the project, about which Sam knew essentially all there was to know, having worked on the project as an interpreter during its exploration and early appraisal phases. He paid much closer attention to her as she described the challenges of building and transporting such a massive structure—by this time they were walking in its shadow, and soon would be immediately beside it. They moved on to a small elevator in which they rode to the "top" of the structure (actually to the highest spot on one of the legs), where Sam had an all-encompassing view of the yard below and the horizon in the distance. He could clearly see and follow the channel through which the facility would be floated out to sea, and he was very glad he had brought his camera.

After being brought back to earth, Sam and Anne went around to the base of the structure where he could get a "bottoms-up" view. She began to tell him about the details of how the structure would be anchored to the seabed but was interrupted by the buzzing of her cell phone. She asked Sam to accompany her to a safe location across the yard, and then excused herself to answer the call.

Sam hadn't been standing alone for more than two or three minutes when a young man, one of the construction workers, walked over to him. His appearance left no doubt that he was a man who worked hard with his hands for a living—he was wearing heavily scuffed steel-toed boots, oil-stained jeans, a thick plaid shirt, leather gloves, and a hard hat that had seen better days (Sam remembers trying to imagine what he must have done to have suffered so much damage to his headgear). For this man, a working lunch did not include the privilege of having his employer pay for his meal.

"Who are you?"

"I'm Sam ———— from the company's Houston office. I'm touring the facility with Anne, the project manager. She's on the phone right now and asked me to wait here. Don't worry, I won't wander off and get myself hurt."

Sam's attempt to make some disarming remark, and his poor choice of safety for his topic, didn't appear to faze the man at all. He continued to look at Sam with an expression whose meaning Sam couldn't interpret.

"What do you have to do with this project?"

"I'm a geoscientist, actually a geophysicist. Several years ago I made some of the maps that led to discovery of the oil field where this facility will be installed."

Sam thought he might say a little more about the geology of the field or his job as an interpreter, but he didn't. Later he'd be embarrassed that he hadn't said more about his work because he'd thought the man wouldn't have understood him.

The man's face brightened noticeably, and he took a step closer to Sam.

"I've never met anyone who does what you do. I want to thank you because if you hadn't done your job, I might not have my job here."

The man turned away and went back to his work, and was soon out of sight behind the structure. Sam hadn't learned anything about his job or even his name. By this time Anne had finished her phone call, and was walking toward Sam to continue with their tour.

There has not been another time in Sam's career when he has been shown more sincere appreciation for his work than on that day in the construction yard. ▶

The morning paper and Sergeant Jimmy Hall

AUGUST 2006

Editor's note: The article referred to in this column, titled "The many, the proud, the grunts," was published in the Houston Chronicle *on 30 October 2005.*

Sam brought his Sunday paper to the office on Monday morning because he hadn't had time to read it at home. This wasn't all that unusual for him; following no logical pattern (every now and then but no more than a few times a month), he would bring his morning paper to the office, even though his normal daily practice involved quickly scanning the headlines on several of the news services available on the Internet. On this day he departed from his routine, perhaps to avoid staring at a screen any more than he absolutely had to, or perhaps to soothe his nostalgia for the times when you didn't have to imbibe every bit of information you needed through some sort of electronic device, or perhaps to simply hold the news in his own hands and feel newsprint instead of plastic keys. He started to read with no specific section of the paper or type of story in mind, and soon came upon an article in the editorial section on the role of noncommissioned officers, referred to colloquially as noncoms or NCOs, in the modern U.S. military establishment. This article, with the subtitle "In praise of the military NCOs who get things done," among other things made a very clear distinction between giving orders and getting things done, and described the NCOs of today as the "heart and soul" of the military, men and women whose duties require them to be both "technical experts and corporate-style managers."

This article captured Sam's interest because, during his time on active duty in the service, he, as a junior officer (a lieutenant), had worked with quite a few NCOs. His relationships with them in superior-subordinate terms had occasionally

> **Sam also had learned, not without considerable discomfort, that being an officer did not guarantee that all his command decisions would be good ones.**

been awkward, because Sam, although an officer, was younger and certainly less experienced than most of the NCOs in his squadron. Fortunately for him, the senior NCOs recognized his situation (they had broken in more than one or two junior officers), and took the initiative to ease Sam into his command position. One of the NCOs that Sam remembered doing this for him was Sergeant Jimmy Hall, an easygoing, affable man who seemed to wear a perpetual smile. It didn't take Sam long to recognize that Sergeant Hall had earned the respect of officers and enlisted men alike. Sam had noticed and admired how he handled the younger enlisted men, boys really, some no more than 18 or 19 years old, bringing them gently but firmly into an adult world of guns, trucks, and doomsday weapons, all in a day's work. At the time Sam didn't realize that in his own way he stood at the doorway to that same world, and that Sergeant Hall would lead him through it.

After having watched Sam struggling for several weeks to adjust to his position in their shop, Sergeant Hall called Sam aside one afternoon to offer some advice.

"Lieutenant, I think you'll get along just fine here if we have an understanding. We (the enlisted men) know that you have to give us orders, or at least it has to look like you're giving us orders. You know by now that we all can do our jobs without being told what to do or how to do it. If you give us the room, we'll get the work done and make you look good at the same time. OK?"

Sam can't recall what he said, if anything, in response to Sergeant Hall. He does remember taking his advice to heart, and as a result being less hesitant to sit down with the NCOs and solicit their opinions on many different subjects. He remembers also that their shop ran very smoothly, more or less in exactly the way Sergeant Hall had described in giving orders and getting things done.

Half a lifetime later, this article now caused Sam to reminisce about Sergeant Hall, not only as a very capable NCO, but also as a man with a firm grasp of human nature. As a younger man and junior officer, Sam had come to his duty station thinking that an officer gives orders because it's his job to give orders, and that he is intrinsically able to make better decisions because of fundamental differences between himself and the enlisted men under his command. Without upsetting their authority structure, Sergeant Hall had helped Sam learn that all kinds of people make good decisions at all levels throughout an entire organization, and that what really matters is gaining common understanding of the roles filled by different individuals within that organization. Sam also had learned, not without considerable discomfort, that being an officer did not guarantee that all his command decisions would be good ones.

Heart and soul—technical expert—getting things done—in another time and place, Sergeant Jimmy Hall might have been a pretty good interpreter. ▶

If the fault is there, then I've missed thousands more like it

OCTOBER 2006

Sam's supervisor asked him to review the mapping of a prospect that was being brought forward for an upcoming lease sale. It was common practice in the company for exploration teams to seek the assistance and advice of experienced interpreters such as Sam as part of the quality assurance process, especially in advance of a lease sale. What was different about this request, as Sam learned when he entered the office of the interpreter who had mapped the prospect, was that only two other people would be in the review: Jerry, the prospect generator, and Pete, Jerry's team leader. Sam wasn't worried about being the only "independent" reviewer; having done this sort of thing before, he wasn't lacking in self-confidence and knew that no matter what he saw or heard, he would honestly and of course tactfully voice his opinions—otherwise, why bother to comment at all? He was somewhat concerned that with an odd number of people in the meeting there might be a tendency to subconsciously take sides, often in anticipation of the most politically desirable outcome, or simply to align one's thinking with the senior person present. Sam wasn't sure how this particular encounter might turn out and silently promised himself that he would be as fair and rational as possible.

Fortunately Sam knew both Jerry and Pete, although he had never worked directly with or for either of them. As soon as they had exchanged greetings, Pete began by briefly going over a few ground rules for the review and the timetable for technical and management meetings leading up to the sale. Jerry started the technical discussion by describing the seismic data used to map the prospect; these data were entirely 2D, the prospect being in one of those few areas that had not yet been covered by a 3D survey. He then presented the details of the prospect in terms of its three primary risk components: trap, reservoir, and source (including both generation and migration of hydrocarbons). It was immediately evident to Sam that the greatest risk for the prospect was trap; two of the prospect's trap edges were defined by faults, in what you might call "trap door" geometry. As Jerry continued, Sam realized that he would necessarily focus his attention on the interpretation of these faults.

When Jerry finished his presentation, Pete asked Sam for his impressions of the prospect and whether or not he had any questions.

"Well, the prospect looks pretty good, based on what you've shown me today. I don't think you have any problems with reservoir presence or quality, and your charge story is consistent with our model for the area. I am concerned about trap risk, because the prospect as mapped depends on two separate faults."

"We feel the same way. We recognize that trap integrity is our greatest risk and have spent a lot of time and effort on our fault interpretation, especially those two faults."

"I'd like to see this line here, line 27," said Sam, pointing to a line crossing one of the two critical faults.

> **" Sam had too much respect for Jerry to say any more and wasn't sure that he hadn't already said too much. "**

Jerry selected line 27 from the map display on his workstation and placed the cursor on the fault in question as Sam carefully looked at the line.

"This interpretation looks good to me, Jerry. Is this line typical of all of the data you used to define this fault?"

"Yes it is. We feel very good about this one."

For an instant Sam wondered if Jerry's remark meant that he might not feel as good about the other fault.

"Great. Let's have a look at a line across the other fault. How about line 14 here?"

Jerry brought up line 14 on his workstation, but this time Sam's reaction wasn't the same as when he saw line 27.

"Could you please move the cursor to that fault," asked Sam, pointing on Jerry's map display to the second of the two critical faults.

Jerry moved the cursor to that fault, and Sam could now clearly see which fault on line 14 corresponded to the critical fault on the map. For a few seconds Sam squinted at the line, because there appeared to be no displacement across the fault; that is, as nearly as Sam could tell, Jerry had driven the fault through a package of continuous reflections that weren't offset at all. He wondered if the fault might not have been interpreted as a strike-slip fault but dismissed that possibility after looking closely at the contours on Jerry's map.

"OK," said Sam hesitantly, "can we look at lines 12 and 16 on either side of line 14?"

"No problem, Sam," and Jerry quickly displayed both lines, each in its own window on the screen. Sam saw that there was a fault on each of these lines exactly as Jerry had mapped, but it wasn't at all obvious that these faults could be correlated from one line to the other. On looking at the structure map again, and remembering that he had seen no credible evidence for faulting on line 14, Sam wondered whether the faults picked on lines 12 and 16 were in fact two separate breaks that should not be correlated as a single fault.

"Have you considered the possibility that the faults you see on lines 12 and 16 are not correlative?" Sam knew that if this were the case, then the prospect would effectively be made too small to be economically viable, if present at all.

"We considered that, but based on our interpretation of line 14, we believe that we can correlate a single fault all the way across the structure."

"It looks to me like you're putting a fault through continuous reflections on line 14 if you do that. Do your data quality and fault correlation criteria in this area support doing this?"

"Yes they do."

"If that's so, then I must have missed thousands, no, tens of thousands of faults just like this one during the course of my career."

Sam had too much respect for Jerry to say any more and wasn't sure that he hadn't already said too much. He hoped that Jerry and Pete had taken his comment in the sense that it was intended—that he considered the fault interpretation to be very risky, if not incorrect.

At this somewhat awkward juncture the three men considered the review to be finished. Pete thanked Sam for his time and asked him to summarize his comments in an e-mail to him with a copy to the exploration manager.

Later that day Sam happened to bump into Jerry in the hallway.

"About my comments on your fault interpretation this morning, Jerry...."

"Don't worry about it, Sam, I know what you were trying to say. We know how it is—once a fault appears on a map, especially if it helps set up a prospect, it takes an act of Congress to change it, much less remove it. And since there aren't very many interpreters elected to Congress these days...."

Chapter 6: 2007

Marginal versus considerable

JANUARY 2007

Sam and Richard, his good friend and the geologist with whom he often partnered on interpretation projects, had recently completed a reservoir study at the request of one of the company's international offices. This study, designed to consolidate a wealth of technical data from one of the company's most lucrative assets, was a combined geoscience-reservoir engineering undertaking in which Sam handled the seismic interpretation and Richard did the core description and analysis as well as log correlations. They integrated their work with that of a small team of engineers, and the final product of their collective efforts was a full 3D flow simulation model of the field.

On completion of their part of the project, Sam and Richard wrote a detailed report in which they documented every aspect of their work. This was particularly demanding for Sam, because one of the most challenging elements of the project for him had been to use seismic inversions for detailed mapping of the reservoir section. The inversions he used were products of the company's newest inversion package, which previously had not been available for business projects. Sam had paid close attention to R&D geophysicists as they described the ins and outs of the inversion software, and in turn they had kept in touch with Sam to see how their results were put to use in an active interpretation. At the same time he was interpreting the inversions, he also was interpreting in parallel the time-migrated reflectivity data from which the inversions were generated; in this way he developed a foundation for comparison (a baseline, if you will) of the relative strengths and weaknesses of both data sets as employed in the project.

As he wrote the project report with this comparison in mind, Sam pondered how to summarize his conclusion about the benefits of using inversions for interpreting the reservoir section. After considerable thought and several false starts, he wrote that interpretation of seismic inversions in this particular project represented a marginal improvement over working with more conventional reflectivity sections. Having finally decided this, Sam thought that he probably had spent too much time worrying about it—after all, he had never been uncertain about his conclusion, only about the words he chose to express it. And, in any case, wasn't the accuracy of his interpretation and its consistency with well control more important than the technology used to achieve his results?

Several days after Sam and Richard submitted a draft of their report, Dave, their supervisor, called them to his office. Dave passed his hand-edited copy of the report to Sam, who quickly flipped through it and was pleasantly surprised to see very little red ink (Dave was old-school in doing his editing with a red pen). But when Sam looked at the summary and conclusions section at the end of the report, he noticed one correction where a single word had been marked through with a slashing red line, a bold stroke that looked almost as though it had been drawn in anger and for maximum effect. The word marked through was "marginal," and it had been replaced with the word "considerable" to describe the improvement realized by using seismic inversions rather than reflectivity data in the project. This

> *The word marked through was 'marginal,' and it had been replaced with the word 'considerable' to describe the improvement realized by using seismic inversions rather than reflectivity data in the project.*

was not a suggested change—it was a mandatory one. The rest of the summary and conclusions section was unmarked.

"Dave, in the summary and conclusions here I see that you want me to change the word marginal to considerable in my assessment of the utility of inversions in this project. I thought about that for some time while writing the report, and I'd rather say that the improvement was marginal because that's what I honestly think."

"I understand, Sam. But there are a lot of people watching this project who have high expectations of our inversion technology. Make the change as I've indicated."

Knowing Dave as he did, Sam could see that more discussion would be pointless, and so he made the change as directed. Interestingly enough, there were very few other edits of any substance elsewhere in the report, and when it was finally approved and distributed, its technical content was essentially unchanged from that of the first draft.

A month or so later, Sam and Richard learned that Dan, the exploration manager who had originally requested the reservoir study, was coming to town. Dave asked them to prepare a presentation of the geoscience portion of the reservoir study for Dan, who himself had worked as a geophysicist earlier in his career. Dave cautioned Sam to be mindful of any comments he might make about using inversions in the project—in fact, he strongly suggested that Sam avoid comparisons of inversions and reflectivity data altogether. The presentation went ahead without controversy, and Dan seemed to be very pleased with Sam and Richard's work.

"Dave, your team has done excellent work here. I'm sure we'll put it to good use back in the district."

Dan then turned directly to Richard.

"I'd like you to come to the district office to give this presentation to my subsurface team…"

Then he faced Sam.

"…but I don't see any reason why you would need to come."

This statement, completely unexpected, visibly upset Richard, and the vacant look on Dave's face, whose eyes were unable to meet Sam's, told Sam everything he needed to know.

The meeting was effectively over, and when Dave and Dan had left the conference room, Richard spoke up.

"Sam, I can't believe what I just heard. We worked together throughout the entire project—how could he expect either one of us alone to accurately present this work and intelligently answer all of the questions his staff might ask? It certainly wouldn't cost that much for both of us to travel to the district."

"I don't know what to say. Oddly enough, Dan being a geophysicist and all, I would have thought he'd want me to come in order to discuss the new inversion technology we used. I just don't know…."

In the truest sense of the words, Sam's disappointment at this turn of events was considerable, not marginal. ◗

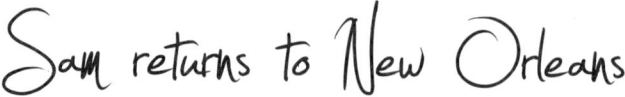

Sam returns to New Orleans

FEBRUARY 2007

Long before he actually left for the airport for his trip to the 2006 Annual Meeting, Sam thought about what he had seen on a half-day business trip to New Orleans earlier in the year. Together with his travel partners, he had driven through one of the areas hit hard by Hurricane Katrina, the Lakeview area (north-northwest of downtown New Orleans on the southern shore of Lake Pontchartrain). What he saw had saddened him—he hadn't been prepared for these sights, and felt diminished by them in an unsettling and unforgettable way. Seeing the extent of the destruction with his own eyes was far different and more deeply moving than the filtered views from the national news networks. The "business as usual" appearance and atmosphere of downtown New Orleans was not sufficiently reassuring for Sam to wipe away his images of other parts of the city.

As was his custom, Sam went to the Icebreaker on Sunday evening. He couldn't imagine what had transpired in the wake of the hurricane one year before in the very building where he was now having a casual drink and renewing acquaintances (later in the week he learned that the SEG Annual Meeting was only the second major event to be held in the Morial Convention Center since it had been restored and opened for business, and even at that several halls within the center still were not open for business). Neither the vendors' displays nor the mood of the attendees, certainly buoyed by good times in the oil and gas industry, gave any hint of the exhibition hall's history of the past year. Sam did notice, or thought he noticed, that students seemed to make up a larger proportion of the overall attendance than they had in Houston the year before. He interpreted this as a good sign for the health of the industry.

Sam didn't attend very many oral presentations, spending the bulk of his time sitting in committee meetings (his "formal" activities) and strolling the floor of the exhibition hall. Walking (or, more accurately, trekking) from the exhibition hall to the far end of the convention center where the oral presentations were held, Sam experienced another real-life example of the meaning of the term "aspect ratio," that is, the Morial Convention Center is very much longer than it is wide. After making this journey two or three times, Sam thought that some moving sidewalks, like those you see in large airports, would be welcome improvements for conventioneers.

> *Could this have been the same mouse, or was it a close relative? If it were the same one, how had it worked its way through the audience to the other end of the platform?*

While skimming through the official program (probably it would have taken an hour or more to carefully read the entire program from cover to cover), Sam decided that he would attend SEG Forum VII, titled "Energy's future: What's different this time?" Previously known as the *TLE* Forum, this event had matured over the past few years to become the de facto introduction to the Annual Meeting's technical program. This year's forum included presentations on alternative energy developments by executives of three major oil companies: Russ Ford of Shell, Don Paul of Chevron, and Terry Wood of BP. Following these presentations, there would be a moderated panel discussion in which the speakers would address questions from the audience. Sam had attended several forums (fora?) before, and thought they had been stimulating and well worth his time.

As with any major effort involving technology and a large number of people, there will be unexpected occurrences, no matter how thorough and vigilant the event planners may be. In the case of an event as large as the SEG Annual Meeting with many presentations occurring in many rooms simultaneously, it would have been folly to think that all of the public address equipment would function flawlessly. So after the forum was under way, Sam was not surprised when the speaker's microphone cut in and out a few times, and for a while the speaker's voice echoed throughout the hall not unlike that of the Great and Powerful Oz in his throne room in the Emerald City. Being very professional, the speakers were not visibly bothered by this, although when the ballroom lights were raised and lowered, several times, to change the illumination of the speakers' platform, no one present could have faulted any of the speakers for being distracted. If all this weren't enough, during Don Paul's presentation the sound system saw fit to issue a sharp feedback buzz that caused most of the people around Sam to jump in their seats. Even Don had to look away for a second to regain his composure, but as moderator Steve Smith said later, Don showed grace under pressure in a situation that might have flustered most other people.

But Sam thinks that neither Don nor Terry noticed what might have been the forum's most unusual distraction, at least to the audience. A few minutes after the loud buzz punctuated Don's presentation, from the vantage point of his front row seat Sam thought he saw a small mouse dart back and forth from under the speaker's platform to a computer monitor directly in front of the platform, on which a speaker could see an image of the slide being projected onto the dual screens behind him (or her). This happened several times, after which the mouse stayed in the greenery arranged around the base of the monitor. Then, during the question and answer session following Don's presentation, the mouse screwed up enough courage to scurry from the cover of the monitor into the front row of the audience, where he disappeared from Sam's view. Sam could only imagine what might have happened had this mouse decided to run up someone's leg, a possibility in the darkened hall.

Toward the end of Terry's presentation Sam happened to look to his right toward the far end of the speaker's platform, where he again saw a mouse run back and forth from under the platform. Could this have been the same mouse, or was it a close relative? If it were the same one, how had it worked its way through the audience to the other end of the platform? We'll never know—but this encore performance continued throughout the latter part of the panel discussion until the mouse returned whence it came, just before the end of the forum—almost as though the mouse was keeping time.

An anonymous source reported that the mouse was actually a robotic device designed, built, and operated by Enders Robinson, but, when asked about this, Enders replied that he knows nothing about mice or any other rodents that attended the forum.

In the aftermath of all this, Sam was reminded of the frequently quoted verse of Robert Burns that "the best-laid plans of mice and men often go awry." Sam thinks that in SEG Forum VII the mice did better than the men. ▶

The top secret Technology Innovation Award

APRIL 2007

Sam returned to his office to find a small handwritten note from his department manager, Tom, asking Sam to come to his office as soon as he had a free moment. This wasn't the first time Tom had communicated with Sam in this fashion—it was part of Tom's laid-back style, and most staff were accustomed to it and actually preferred to be dealt with in this way, as long as the degree of informality was in reasonable proportion to the gravity of the message. In this case Sam wasn't at all anxious about the note, because he hadn't heard any rumors of impending reorganizations or office moves, and certainly the business climate wasn't ripe for a layoff (or force reduction or staffing reconciliation or purge or any other kind of company-sponsored group activity). Sam was slightly concerned, however, because knowing Tom as he did, he thought he sensed some urgency in the note.

Tom greeted Sam warmly as he stepped into his office, and Sam didn't fail to notice that Tom was wearing a "cat that swallowed the canary" smile as he motioned for Sam to sit down.

"You're probably wondering why I asked you to come by, Sam. Don't worry, I don't have any bad news for you—in fact, I have some very good news. You've heard about the company's Technology Innovation Awards Program, haven't you?"

Sam nodded in assent. He thought about how his co-workers jokingly called this program the *TIA*, in reference to the medical term *transient ischemic attack*, that is, a small stroke, which an employee can suffer because it is such a shock to actually receive one of these technology awards.

> *These words were barely out of Sam's mouth before he and Richard were shaking hands and literally jumping up and down like schoolboys.*

"I'm very pleased to tell you that you've been selected for an award in this year's program for your work on the Whoozit Field Reservoir Project. Congratulations, Sam!"

Tom handed Sam an envelope containing a letter from the company's CEO of Exploration and Production and a check for a not insignificant amount of money.

"Thanks very much, Tom. I don't know what to say—I certainly never expected this."

"You earned it, Sam. The company really appreciates your dedication and commitment. Keep up the good work. Oh, by the way—please don't say anything to anyone about your award yet."

Sam walked back to his office in somewhat of a daze, contemplating his good fortune and imagining his wife's reaction to this unforeseen windfall. But as he sat down at his desk, he started to wonder about Tom's having asked him not to say anything about his award. This became increasingly troublesome because he had not worked alone on the Whoozit Project; he had been part of a three-man team comprised of himself, his geologist friend Richard, and a reservoir engineer named Al.

Sam couldn't sit still for more than a few minutes, and then, in spite of what Tom had said, he went to Richard's office.

"Hey, Richard, I was just passing by. What's new?"

"Not much, Sam, more of the same. We haven't really talked since we finished the Whoozit Project, so we do have some catching up to do. Anything new with you?"

There was a nuance in his manner that betrayed Richard—something was up, and Sam couldn't help but wonder if Richard hadn't been to Tom's office as well.

"Did Tom call you into his office this morning?"

"Yes. Why do you ask?"

"He called me in too. Did he give you something?"

"Yes he did."

"Was it a TIA for the Whoozit Project?"

These words were barely out of Sam's mouth before he and Richard were shaking hands and literally jumping up and down like schoolboys. To them, these awards were their due, the fitting conclusion to their project, the recognition that all geoscientists seek and treasure when finally received. One of these makes hundreds of hours of effort worth it, thought Sam.

Then he and Richard were visited by a common thought—what about Al?

"We need to talk to Al."

"But Tom asked us, or me at least, not to say anything to anyone about this."

"That didn't keep you from coming to see me, did it?"

The two men quickly walked to Al's office, which was in a different wing of the building. When they got there, Al was sitting at his desk poring over an engineering textbook of some sort. As he looked up, Sam thought he saw something in Al's face that suggested he had a secret he was dying to tell.

"Well, I haven't seen you two birds for a while. What brings you this way?"

"We just wanted to pay a friendly visit to our favorite reservoir engineer, ha, ha, actually the only reservoir engineer we know."

"You're way too clever to come all the way over here without having an ulterior motive. Let's have it."

"Al, we were wondering if anything unexpected or out of the ordinary has happened to you lately, here in the office."

"Lately—you mean like today?"

"Yes, OK, today or maybe yesterday."

Al paused, looked down for a few seconds and then back up at Sam and Richard.

"This morning I was given a TIA for my work on the Whoozit Field Reservoir Project."

And the scene that had played out in Richard's office a few minutes earlier was now recreated in Al's office, as the three men congratulated each other and began to reminisce about the good times they'd shared on the Whoozit Project. Their laughter was in sharp contrast to the anger and confusion they had also felt during the project, but those sentiments had retreated into the deeper recesses of their memories, from which they would not now be recalled to cloud the present. As they finished their impromptu celebration, they promised to treat themselves to an expensive lunch later in the week.

To the best of Sam's recollection, there never was any notice of their awards for the Whoozit Field Reservoir Project in any of the company's publications, nor were they ever mentioned in any of the department meetings that Sam attended. ▸

The evolution of the new-hire field trip

JUNE 2007

Sam was fortunate enough to have been selected to go on a field trip that was part of the company's new-hire training program. As a senior geoscientist, he would serve as one of the trip guides/instructors, and he would be responsible for leading discussions at several field stops and also commenting in general on geophysics in the field, for example, by describing seismic acquisition instrumentation and techniques or by sketching the theoretical seismic response of an observed geologic feature. The field area was two full days' drive from the company's offices, and so the trip was planned to last for one week, with stops along the way and the appropriate number of overnight stays. Usually there were about 20–25 participants in all, including guides, and so there were always more

> *Sam had learned to recognize such a question as the precursor to an argument, usually a highly emotional one during which no intellectual ground was gained and no minds were ever changed.*

than enough logistical details to worry about, not the least of which was to ensure that a sufficient quantity of safety equipment was taken along for the hiking and climbing that were part of the trip.

One of the most geologically and philosophically (if you will) interesting stops on the trip was the one at which a major angular unconformity could be seen in a very well exposed outcrop. This site was scheduled as the second to the last stop on the third day, and definitely was the highlight of that day, if not of the entire trip. The discussion leader at this stop, who on this occasion was one of the company's most senior geologists, took advantage of the brilliant weather of the day, and the unexpected circumstance that the trip actually was running ahead of schedule, to wax poetic about the grandeur of the processes that created the magnificent unconformity they were now so privileged to stand before. He invited each member of his audience to step forward and place his or her hand across this unconformity, and to marvel at the thought of how the insignificant distance between thumb and little finger would span hundreds of millions of years of geologic time. After such a momentous oration, which the experienced geoscientists such as Sam had expected by way of tradition at this site, the remaining stop and the drive to their lodgings for the night would be a colorless anticlimax.

When they arrived at their motel, Sam waited along with everyone else (students and guides alike) for the trip leader to announce the room assignments for the night. The trip was organized so that two participants shared a double room, with different pairings for each day of the trip unless some special condition or request warranted otherwise. Sam soon learned that his roommate would be Ron, one of the new-hire geologists. He remembered Ron as being very enthusiastic, one of the first off the bus to hike off the road or climb an outcrop. He recalled also that Ron seemed to have been particularly enamored by the unconformity they had seen that afternoon.

Sam and Ron hauled their field gear and overnight bags to their room, and upon entering, Sam immediately went to the bath area to get cleaned up, while Ron nonchalantly turned on the television. As he was washing his face, Sam could hear Ron changing the television channels, and as he was drying his hands he thought he heard a voice from the television saying something about Charles Darwin and evolution. Sam thought that Ron must have tuned to the local public television station, which probably was airing a science program of some sort. As he turned around, Sam saw Ron staring intently, almost threateningly, at the television, or, more accurately, at the man on the television who was talking about Charles Darwin. A few seconds passed, and then Ron looked directly at Sam.

"Can you believe they teach that stuff to our children in school?"

Ron's question was put to Sam in very much of an accusatory tone, as though anything but the right answer simply would not be tolerated. Sam had learned to recognize such a question as the precursor to an argument, usually a highly emotional one during which no intellectual ground was gained and no minds were ever changed.

"Teach what?"

"Evolution, of course. What this fellow on the TV is talking about as though it were fact."

Sam knew that whatever he said next would most likely determine how the rest of the evening would go—and, as luck would have it, just as he was preparing as innocuous a response as he could muster, there was a knock at the door. Through the door he heard the voice of his good friend Jack, who also was one of the trip guides.

"Hey, are you guys in there or not? We're getting ready to go to dinner. Come on, open up!"

Given this reprieve, Sam moved quickly to open the door, and in walked Jack and Mark, the new hire he was rooming with that night.

"Say, what's on TV? Is there any news to be had in this small town?" asked Mark.

Sam tried to motion to Jack and Mark that they should leave right away, but he was not successful.

"There's some fellow going on about evolution—you wouldn't believe some of the things he's saying," said Ron.

"Oh really?" answered Mark.

By this time Sam had managed to pull Jack out of the room and was herding him down the walkway toward the restaurant adjacent to their motel.

"What was going on in there, Sam? Why did you hustle me out so quickly? Are we going to leave Mark and Ron?"

"I think we should just be on our way to dinner. I was very nearly roped into an argument that I didn't want to be in, either today or on any other day."

"What argument do you mean?"

"Well, Ron had tuned to a television channel on which there was a discussion of evolution and Charles Darwin, and apparently he was angry that evolution is taught in our schools."

"So what's the big deal? He's a geoscientist, like you and me, or at least he says he is, so why should he have a problem with that?"

"I don't know. I do remember that he seemed to be quite interested in the unconformity we saw today and the concept of geologic time as we discussed it, but maybe that was only my impression and doesn't reflect what was going on in his head."

"Who knows, Sam, if any of us can really tell what's going on in someone else's head?"

"Jack, I've heard it said that one measure of intelligence is the ability to hold two conflicting thoughts in one's mind at the same time."

"If that's so, then our young friend Ron may be one of the most intelligent people we'll ever know." ▶

Paul's exit interview

SEPTEMBER 2007

For Sam the morning started out like most other mornings—the short walk from the parking garage to the office tower, the elevator ride to his floor, stopping to put his lunch in the refrigerator in the break area, unlocking the door to his office, taking his PC out of the cabinet and locking it into the docking station, powering up both the PC and his workstation, and looking out of his window at the stream of unfortunates creeping along the freeway treadmill to pinpoint destinations on the horizon. This morning he would review his e-mail as usual, but he also would take a few extra minutes to check the company's opening stock price and read the electronic news, especially to see how the local professional sports team had fared the evening before. Usually this was quiet time, because most of the time Sam was the first on his floor to arrive for work.

He had finished reading the news and been logged in to his interpretation project for no more than 15 or 20 minutes when his good friend Jack poked his head into Sam's office.

"Did you hear what just happened?"

Jack was one of those who took great delight in being the first to pass on a good rumor or real news—it didn't matter which.

"No. What could already have happened this early in the morning?"

"Paul just quit. Dave (Paul's supervisor, and also Jack's and Sam's) hadn't been in his office for more than 30 seconds—he probably hadn't even hung up his coat yet—when Paul just marched in, plunked down his letter of resignation, and walked out. You know Paul, a man of few words. Dave never had the time to make a counteroffer."

Sam snickered at Jack's last remark, because knowing Paul as he did, he was certain there was nothing Dave or anyone else in the company could do or say that would have caused him to change his mind. They used to talk about what they would or wouldn't do on the day they quit, and one of the unbreakable rules was that once you put the paper down, you didn't pick it up—the time for negotiation would have passed long before.

"So where is Paul going?"

"I haven't spoken with him yet, so I don't really know. There are some rumors, but we should probably just ask him directly. You know what the company tradition is—he'll have an exit interview, clean out his office, turn in his security pass, and be gone by noon. We'll take him out to lunch, and he'll tell us then."

And so it happened. Sam and Jack helped Paul carry several boxes of books and other personal possessions to his car and then walked a few blocks down the street to their favorite sandwich shop. This restaurant, if it could be called that (for it really wasn't a very glamorous place), was a favorite of Sam's peer group, partly because of the quality of the food (above average on the worst of days) and partly because of its atmosphere, even though on most of their visits Sam and his friends ate at an outside table, space and weather permitting. On the inside, the shop's most memorable features were the sights and smells of the serving line,

> *Why do they ask the people who have already quit and not those of us who are still here?*

where some of the roughest men Sam had ever seen filled orders. These men, half of whom were said to be working there as a condition of parole, exchanged hard stares with customers if they bothered to look at them. Their physical appearance, dominated by their broad chests and sinewed arms (often decorated with tattoos that would embarrass the average professional basketball player), was strangely compromised by the hair nets they wore to comply with the city's health code. But the smells wafting from the trays of food more than offset any hesitation one might feel in their presence—they served the best quarter-pound hamburger with fries in the neighborhood. Sam and his friends had come to look forward to eating there, and they never thought twice about recommending the shop to others.

Sam, Jack, and Paul picked up their usual lunchtime fare and sat down at one of the sidewalk tables.

"So where are you going, Paul?"

"I've taken a position at Colossal Oil, in their new offices on the east side of town. They were filling a regional geophysicist position, and I fit right into their plans. Their benefits package is much better, and their offer included a double-digit increase in my base salary and a healthy signing bonus to boot. My commute will be a few miles shorter, and they actually subsidize carpooling in a meaningful way, as though they're really committed to it."

"Sounds great to me. How do I get on board there?"

They all laughed at this, but Sam sensed that Jack wasn't too comfortable at that particular moment.

"How did your exit interview go?"

"Well, the HR guy asked me all the standard questions about why I was leaving and whether I was getting a higher salary. I'm not sure he was really concerned about my reasons for leaving, especially since he's an HR type who has no earthly idea about what geophysicists do, other than what he sees in pictures in the company magazine. He did ask me what I thought the company could do to keep talented people like me from leaving."

At this, Jack became visibly angry and threw his sandwich down on his plate.

"Why are they asking you? As though HR can do something about it? Why do they ask the people who have already quit and not those of us who are still here?"

"If my father were here, he'd call that closing the barn door after the horse ran out. But it does make you wonder whether the horse wouldn't run out if someone put more feed in the barn." ▸

Mistakes on the slides

OCTOBER 2007

Sam scanned his calendar and was delighted to see that he had only one meeting scheduled for the day, and that was his supervisor Dave's regular biweekly staff meeting. Sam actually looked forward to this meeting, because among Dave's talents was his ability to conduct a meeting well: start on time, ensure all participants know each other, stick to the agenda circulated before the meeting, manage questions, keep discussion on topic, conclude with a concise statement of decisions made and actions to be taken (being specific about who would do what by when), end on time, and distribute written minutes as soon as possible after the meeting (sounds so much like common sense, doesn't it?).

On this day, among the more mundane items on the agenda, Dave himself was going to repeat a presentation he had given the week before to senior management, in which he summarized a technical project completed by his team and the business recommendations made on the basis of that work. Sam was very interested in seeing this presentation because he had provided quite a few maps and sections for Dave to use in putting his talk together, but he never had a chance to see the final product. This wasn't a problem for Sam because he trusted Dave to accurately represent his work; but Sam had been singed before by others who had "borrowed" his material, and he had learned after the fact that some of these people had used it to suit their own ends and not necessarily acknowledged him or presented his methods and conclusions as he would have. These circumstances were not so much questions of accuracy but rather of intent—in describing the results of an interpretation, Sam knew only too well how easy it is to influence decision-makers by the manner in which technical analyses and uncertainty are presented.

Dave had proceeded only as far as the second slide in his talk when Sam recognized some of his material. This slide, which illustrated the structural setting of the project area, consisted of a depth-migrated seismic line with an inset structure map showing the location of the line. Although the inset map was quite small, it was still large enough to be examined in some detail. Sam noticed that the location of the displayed line was misplaced on this map; that is, if one were to draw a cross section from the map for the location of the line as shown, it would not match the seismic section it was supposed to represent. Sam was concerned because the amount of mispositioning was significant and did not appear to be simply a drafting error. When Dave paused for a moment in his presentation, having not yet moved on to his next slide, Sam spoke up.

"Dave, it looks like the location of the seismic section as shown on the inset map on that slide is not right. The line of the section needs to be moved over to the left and rotated a little bit in order for the seismic section to match the structure as shown on the map. Either that, or we've used the wrong seismic section for that slide."

"You may be right, Sam, but it really doesn't matter at this scale or for the purpose of the slide. I'm only establishing the structural context for our project, and that level of detail isn't important."

> *...Sam had been singed before by others who had 'borrowed' his material, and he had learned after the fact that some of these people had used it to suit their own ends...*

That explanation will have to do, thought Sam, although he wondered why Dave hadn't asked him to review his slides before the presentation to management—he would have seen that mistake right away, and he could have fixed it so that anyone who might use the same slide some other time wouldn't be further distributing misinformation. Drop it for now, he thought, and get with the technical assistant to make the correction later.

Dave had moved on to his third slide, which consisted of a bulleted list of topics to be discussed in the body of the presentation. As Dave spoke, individual line items on the slide zipped or whooshed into view, each accompanied by its own distinct sound effect. Sam was always amused by this presentation technique (or gimmick, you might call it), but he had seen it used so many times that he'd become used to it and was no longer distracted by it.

After a few more minutes, Dave showed a slide comparing the original and reprocessed depth imaging of the 3D data in the project area. Sam thought this was a very important slide because he had been able to interpret with much greater confidence on the reprocessed data, and he had taken a lot of time to carefully select the line Dave was using for comparison in his slide. But Sam paused—he knew there were two versions of reprocessing, each using different migration algorithms, and then remembered that he had given Dave three seismic snapshots, one of the original processing and one of each reprocessed version. There were only two images on Dave's slide, and as Sam looked more closely, he saw that the reprocessed image on the slide had been mislabeled as having been migrated with the algorithm actually used for the version not shown. Sam could hardly wait to bring this to Dave's attention.

"Dave, it looks to me like the reprocessed depth image shown on the right side of that slide is really the version for which we used our ABCD migration algorithm, but it's labeled as having been migrated with our WXYZ algorithm. That's a very important distinction that needs to be made correctly, because anyone else who sees this could get the impression that we're recommending using the WXYZ approach in this type of setting, whereas we're actually saying that the ABCD algorithm works better here."

"Are you sure about that, Sam?"

"Absolutely. I've spent as much time as anyone looking at these data, and I can verify this on the workstation and with our data processing group if you'd like."

"Well, in any case it doesn't matter all that much. That level of detail isn't important—what's more important is that we convey the message that the depth imaging needs to be tailored specifically to the problem at hand."

"But don't you think that we should be sure to inform the people who saw these slides that we really mean to recommend using the ABCD algorithm in this area?"

Sam felt himself moving perilously close to the brink of self-destruction but kept on. "We don't want to propagate misinformation throughout the company, do we? This is only a matter of saying that there's a mistake on the slide."

"Next slide, please." ▶

Sam visits San Antonio

NOVEMBER 2007

Attending this year's SEG Annual Meeting was Sam's first trip to San Antonio since 2001, the year in which the meeting was last held in the Alamo City. Although the painful memories of shock and disbelief at the events of 11 September 2001 may never fade, they are softened by the enduring testimony of truly selfless acts throughout the world that followed the tragedy.

For his part, Sam had heard secondhand about the generosity of many companies and individuals at the Annual Meeting in arranging or providing transportation for those not able to return to their homes because of the disruption of commercial airline service. Sam actually was not in San Antonio on that day, having opted to participate only in a Continuing Education course on the weekend before and not to attend the full meeting.

On the morning of the 11th, he was in his office as usual, hard at work forcing a pick through some uninterpretable subsalt data, when one of his team members came in to tell him that he had heard on his radio that a plane had crashed into one of the World Trade Center towers. How can this be, he thought—have we finally uncovered one of the hidden flaws in our 21st-century air traffic control system?

Sam recalled the story of a foggy morning in New York City in July 1945 when a providentially unarmed B-25 bomber struck the Empire State Building, killing 14 people, and he imagined that the casualties from this accident would be far worse. The news that reached him soon after brought the ominous realization that two plane crashes within minutes and a fraction of a mile of each other were not accidents, and it would be evident in the following hours that casualties would be orders of magnitude greater than those 56 years before. The stories of the World Trade Center set firmly and unforgettably in Sam's mind the jarring contrast between the heartless worst and compassionate best we can be, leaving unanswered the fundamental question of what we really mean by civilization and humanity.

As Sam crossed a short bridge over the River Walk on the first day of the meeting, he wasn't thinking about September 11th; rather, he was admiring the inviting appearance of the Henry B. Gonzalez Convention Center. To Sam's eye, this facility was not a typical contemporary design, that is, a sharply angular composition of concrete with brightly painted steel and glass, but one with muted colors, not too

> **"*The stories of the World Trade Center set firmly and unforgettably in Sam's mind the jarring contrast between the heartless worst and compassionate best we can be, leaving unanswered the fundamental question of what we really mean by civilization and humanity.*"**

much glass and a light touch of southwestern style (Sam is no architect, but he knows what he likes).

You might say that Sam was not as impressed with the interior as with the exterior, but he thought it was much easier to find his way around in this building than in the New Orleans convention center. He had forgotten about (or never seen) the gallery of life-size bronze statues of famous Texans in the convention center, and he had not known that Ed White, one of the three Apollo astronauts killed in a launch pad fire in 1967, was a San Antonio native.

The exhibit hall (or in this case the array of interconnected halls) was as spectacular as usual—each year the displays seem to have evolved into more intricate or imposing forms, and here one cannot unreasonably expect to find a real example or virtual representation of any geophysical equipment or service related to the oil and gas business. This year, with the price per barrel of oil having topped US$80, it seemed as though the height of some of the pavilions was directly proportional to that price. Among the most eye-catching sights on the exhibition floor were the green shirts worn by the numerous representatives of one the geophysical service companies (which will go nameless here to avoid commercialism or any implication of endorsement). Sam struggled to find the right adjective to describe this particular shade of green, but he could only come up with pungent, which, although customarily associated with taste or smell, does seem to capture the visual intensity of these shirts. Sam considers their effect to be a genuine triumph of advertising.

Sam has been interpreting seismic data long enough and with sufficient peaks and valleys in his experience that he can honestly say he's seen seismic data in his sleep, and also has seen them in some out-of-the-way places, one of which involved drying developed analog shot records in the desert sun on the hood of a truck. But he certainly didn't expect to see a seismic line where he saw one at this meeting, affixed to the side of one of the buses transporting people to and from the convention center (this also was a clever advertising idea by another service company).

Never having been the type to pass by an interesting seismic line, Sam had to stop and stare at this one, which was about 20 feet long and fully interpreted with at least a dozen horizons and many faults (by its length and scale you could tell it was a regional line). From a distance, Sam thought he saw the same line on all of the buses, and he wondered if anyone had thought of putting a different line on each bus and then running an interpretation contest of some sort based on the set of "bus lines." Would you have had to correctly jump correlate from bus to bus in order to win?

As has become his habit, on Monday morning Sam attended the SEG Forum, this year titled "Unconventional Resources." Of the four speakers, each of whom gave excellent presentations, Sam thought that Larry Lunardi, vice president of geophysics for Chesapeake Energy Corporation, provided the deepest and most entertaining insights into this fascinating topic.

Focusing mostly on gas plays associated with the Barnett, Woodford, and Fayetteville shales in the United States Midcontinent, he discussed technical details of the seismic programs that are critical to Chesapeake's successful pursuit of these plays. Their most unique program was acquisition of a 3D survey covering Dallas-Forth Worth International Airport, and Lunardi illustrated the challenges of this survey with a remarkable picture of two vibroseis trucks parked on the tarmac no more than what appeared to be a few tens of yards from a commercial jet. Sam had no trouble visualizing the quizzical expressions on the faces of passengers looking out of the terminal windows at these strange vehicles sitting next to "their" aircraft. It was no surprise to Sam that many of the questions put to the forum panelists were directed to Lunardi.

Sam was on careful watch throughout this year's forum and did not see any mice in attendance. ◗

Chapter 7: 2008

The offer he couldn't refuse

JANUARY 2008

Sam's supervisor asked him to come to the weekly meeting of the exploration management team. This invitation came as no surprise to Sam—several times he had asked his supervisor, Dave, if he could attend this meeting, for the simple reason that he was interested in seeing how high-level exploration decisions are made. He thought, for right or wrong, that he wouldn't be out of place in the meeting because he felt he had earned the right to sit in by virtue of his years of experience with the company. Sam had given a presentation at this meeting on more than a few occasions, but he had never been allowed to witness any business proceedings other than those to which his presentations were directly related. Even in view of confidentiality and the need for security of information, Sam had always felt excluded and even a bit embarrassed when he, and usually he alone, was politely asked to leave the meeting so that the implicitly more important business could be done.

While thinking about going to the management meeting, Sam remembered Howard, a geologist for whom he had worked in one of his previous assignments. As a team leader, Howard had a reputation for being very straightforward (some called him blunt, others outspoken, still others irresponsible). Once on their way home from the office (Howard and Sam often shared a ride), Sam had asked Howard about a management committee meeting that had taken place that day. Howard was visibly upset by something that had happened in that meeting, but he chose not to go into specific detail; rather, he spoke to Sam in general terms.

"You know, Sam, there are times when I really don't understand our decision-making process. Today we rubber-stamped an AFE for a well totaling several tens of millions of dollars, with virtually no discussion. Then we spent almost an hour haggling over one small part of the evaluation program for the same well, which at several tens of thousands of dollars is a pittance compared to the overall well cost. It's as though we argue only about amounts of money that we really understand, that have concrete feel to them, that you could hold in your hand—for instance, the several tens of thousands of dollars I just mentioned is about the same amount of money that some people you and I know would pay for a late-model luxury car."

"You're probably right—I don't know anyone who has ever held tens of millions of dollars in his hand."

In any case, Sam was thinking about Howard and wondering what weighty matters of budget and other profundities would be discussed in the meeting as he took his seat in an inconspicuous corner of the conference room ("keep your back to the wall and one eye on the door" came to mind as a semi-serious meeting mantra he had once heard). He noticed that the meeting participants seemed to be entering the room in reverse order of importance, that is, the most senior individuals were the last to come in. There also seemed to be much concern about who sat where, but Sam was never able to figure out the exact meaning of the final seating arrangement. One of the company's senior vice presidents, Bob, who from his earliest days as an exploration geologist had risen through the ranks to

> ❝ *To say that people were shocked, dumbfounded, or bewildered by this completely unexpected announcement would serve only to betray the failure of language to describe the surge of feelings that swept across the conference room.* ❞

his current position, would chair the meeting. Bob enjoyed a very good reputation with nearly all of his staff as both a technically sound and financially astute manager, and Sam anticipated watching him in action.

Bob rose from his seat to open the meeting.

"Good morning, everyone, and thank you all for coming. As the first order of business, I'll ask Dave to chair this meeting and excuse myself. You see, I've tendered my resignation, effective immediately, and in the interest of all concerned think it's best that I not participate in this meeting. I'm leaving the company because I was given an offer I couldn't refuse, and I took it."

And with that Bob strode purposefully from the room.

To say that people were shocked, dumbfounded, or bewildered by this completely unexpected announcement would serve only to betray the failure of language to describe the surge of feelings that swept across the conference room. For what seemed like 10 minutes (it was really not much more than a few seconds, the time it took for the sound of Bob's footsteps in the hall to fade away) no one said a word or made any move, other than to settle just a bit lower in his chair, and then Dave spoke. Sam won't soon forget how his respect for Dave increased as he watched him handle this most difficult of situations.

"We'll proceed with the agenda for the meeting as planned. In view of this development with Bob, please be sure not to lose your focus on the business at hand, and certainly don't start or be party to any rumors. I'm sure we'll learn more about this in very short order."

Dave then proceeded with the meeting, and as far as Sam could tell there were some discussions and decisions not unlike those Howard had mentioned. But Sam didn't listen carefully, if at all, to the business of this meeting he had so much wanted to attend. He was daydreaming about what he would do and say in the office on the day when he announced that he had taken an offer he couldn't refuse. ▶

Right at the wrong time

MARCH 2008

A man thinking or working is always alone, let him be where he will.
—Henry David Thoreau

Sam was still awake when Dave began discussion of the last item on the agenda for his biweekly group meeting. This particular topic, the reconfiguration of offices to the so-called open plan, had been controversial before, and today, when the final schedule for construction and associated moves was to be announced, promised to be no exception. Sam had been particularly vocal in his disagreement with the company's pronouncements that the new office plan would foster collaboration among the staff and ultimately result in greater efficiency and more thorough integration of the different subsurface disciplines. He honestly believed that individual offices addressed the interpreter's critical need for privacy, or at least minimum distraction or disruption, whether in the old world of drafting table and paper sections or in the contemporary workstation environment. He knew from experience that interpretation is intensely personal and involves individual style and approach ("there can only be one hand on the mouse at a time"), and that interpreters hadn't been hesitant in the past to call meetings or arrange work sessions when seeking second opinions or peer reviews. He had argued that as an interpreter he didn't want special treatment, only decent treatment that addressed the particulars of his workspace as related to the nature of his job; he had once said that when designing a building, an architect certainly takes into account specific requirements for different spaces in the building based on the tasks to be accomplished in those spaces.

Sam was at the ready when Dave finished his presentation of the schedule for reconfiguration and asked if there were any questions (he might have been better off to have simply ended the meeting, but he was trying to be open with his team and give people a chance to have their say). Sam again repeated his argument for keeping individual offices and then challenged Dave's statement that the move to the open plan was intended to build on the company's recent success.

"I don't understand how this move can be cast as building on our exploration and production success. Isn't it really just one more way to cut costs?"

"No, we think that the new plan really will increase our workplace efficiency and so enable us to grow the success we've realized over the past several years."

As Sam listened to Dave, he noticed that Ed, the most senior member of the subsurface team, was staring intently at him. Almost imperceptibly, Ed was nodding his head from side to side, but his eyes never moved, as though his entire body pivoted around them. Sam was his target, and he had locked onto him. He was transmitting a very clear signal to Sam, a powerful nonverbal message, which from parent to child in a family situation would be translated as "stop what you're doing, right now."

Once he had met Ed's gaze, Sam decided that he had said enough, and he didn't respond to Dave's last remark about the open plan. For his part, Dave realized

> *But why can't we be told straight up that the reconfiguration is simply about costs instead of being cajoled with ideas about efficiency and collaboration? I'd much rather hear that directly, without mincing words, in the same way that we're supposed to communicate the results of our interpretations.*

that he should close the discussion before someone said something he didn't mean, and he mercifully adjourned the meeting. People left the conference room immediately, no one lingering to exchange comments or share small talk; a theater disgorging a crowd of irritated patrons who had just endured an unexpectedly bad movie never emptied so quickly.

Sam knew that he was the source of unnecessary friction on the matter of the open plan, but he couldn't help himself—every time the subject arose he zeroed in on it, no matter where he was or who his audience might be. He was returning to his office when he felt a light touch at his elbow and turned to see Ed at his side. Ed was gently steering Sam toward his office and clearly had something to say.

"Sam, you have to learn how to restrain yourself when this business about the open plan comes up. By now everyone on the team and perhaps everyone in the company knows how you feel, and that you're sincere about it. But enough is enough—nothing you can say is going to change what's going to happen. A corporate decision has been made, and that's that."

"But why can't we be told straight up that the reconfiguration is simply about costs instead of being cajoled with ideas about efficiency and collaboration? I'd much rather hear that directly, without mincing words, in the same way that we're supposed to communicate the results of our interpretations."

"I wouldn't be so sure about that last statement, Sam...but I think you should say no more about the open plan, at any time or in any place."

"But why? How would you ever hope to have any chance to work for something in which you believe, if you don't feel free to argue for your point of view? You don't think I'm wrong about this, do you?"

" It doesn't matter what I think, but I will give you some advice. Over time I've learned that there are two ways to be wrong. The first is to be just plain wrong, you know, two-plus-two-equals-five wrong. The second, and the much more dangerous of the two, is to be right at the wrong time." ▶

How to get a workstation upgrade

JUNE 2008

Sam was packing up in preparation for moving to a new office. This seemed to be a regular, almost seasonal activity at his company, and Sam often wondered what might be the business purpose underlying these moves and their associated interruptions and discomforts. Having survived more than just a few moves within and between different buildings, he had managed to reconcile himself to their inevitability with the thought that from his perch on a relatively low branch of the organizational tree, he must not be high enough to see all of the forest through which the company could successfully pass only by way of frequently moving offices.

Sam had learned to accept an office move as a good opportunity to clean up and out. Over the space of months he, like any other geoscientist, would have accumulated a collection of reports, maps, notebooks, memoranda, unlabeled or obsolete tape cartridges and discs, office supplies, and any number of otherwise half-useless items that he no longer needed to haul around (and might not have either room or use for in his new surroundings). This time, the most notable artifacts he found in his desk were several bottles of dried-up correction fluid, a broken electric eraser, a bundle of colored pencils (on most of which the erasers had been completely rubbed away), and a stack of precisely folded maps from a project he'd worked on many years ago and until now couldn't bear the thought of discarding.

As he carefully packed his personal items into a cardboard box, Sam glanced at his workstation. This machine, in front of which he had spent countless hours, was the L-500 model of the particular brand provided by the vendor with whom the company had its corporate workstation contract. It was not the latest model of that brand (that would be the so-called M-1000 model), but it had always been sufficiently powerful and reliable for Sam to do his work. Sam had seen demonstrations of the M-1000, and he had admired it in the same way one would gaze at a new car through a showroom window; he was on the list for an upgrade to the M-1000, but it seemed like he'd been on the list since the days of reel-to-reel tape drives. As he looked at his L-500, he remembered that he was not supposed to disconnect any of its cabling because the IT people would do that. All he had to do was put adhesive labels on the monitors, keyboard, and tower. When he had finished sealing his boxes, he went ahead and labeled his workstation as instructed and then, as he walked toward the door, without thinking, he gently, almost affectionately, patted the top of the tower.

The following Monday, Sam went to his new office and found to his great surprise and satisfaction that none of his boxes had been lost in the move. He did notice, however, that affixed to one of his workstation's monitors was a yellow Post-It note which read "Do not power up your workstation, call Wayne in IT at extension 2457." Immediately, Sam called Wayne to find out if there was a problem with his workstation.

"Wayne, this is Sam ————. I moved to a new office over the weekend, and this morning found a note on my workstation that said I should call you."

Chapter 7: 2008   87

> **"** *The following Monday, Sam went to his new office and found to his great surprise and satisfaction that none of his boxes had been lost in the move.* **"**

"Oh, yes, Sam ————. We moved you on Saturday. I have some bad news for you. Someone inadvertently bumped or jarred your workstation's tower while unloading it and must have damaged it somehow. We weren't able to power it up."

"Wayne, what am I supposed to do? I need this workstation to do my job."

"Well, if you don't mind we could bring you another one, but all we have are M-1000s. Would one of those be OK?"

"I guess so." Sam could hardly believe what he had heard.

Within an hour, Wayne came to Sam's office with an M-1000, and, after removing the old L-500, hooked up the new machine and ran a few diagnostic tests to be sure it was operating properly.

"You're ready to go, Sam. Hope you like it. Call me if you have any problems."

As Wayne was leaving, he passed Sam's good friend Jack, who was coming by to see how Sam had fared in the move.

"Good morning, Sam! How'd it go with you? They lost only two of my boxes—should find them before too long … what's this, a new workstation, an M-1000? Did they move it in here by mistake? Don't let them have it back, Sam!"

"You won't believe it, Jack, but this is my new workstation. Apparently they broke my old L-500 during the move, dropped it or kicked it or something, and they gave me this new M-1000 as a replacement."

"What, did you bribe the IT guys? They don't just give these away. I've had several birthdays pass since I went on the waiting list for an M-1000 and may never get one—they'll be giving N-2000s or whatever to new hires before I get an M-1000."

"This is all the result of an accident, and I'm not going to question my good fortune."

"Sam, do you think we're going to move again any time soon?" ▶

Criticizing other interpreters

AUGUST 2008

Sam attended a partners' meeting for the first formal review of ongoing interpretations in the agreed technical work program for a newly acquired concession. Brian, one of the company's more experienced geophysicists and the leader of the geoscience team assigned to this project, would begin the meeting with a summary of the company's interpretation. Each of the partners would follow Brian with a technical presentation, and the meeting would conclude with a brief discussion of several commercial business items. Paul, the company's exploration manager for the area in which the concession was located, chaired the meeting.

Brian was a very good speaker, well organized and not one to waste words. His presentations always were clearly illustrated, and Sam could not remember him ever having shown a slide for which he needed to apologize, the kind for which a speaker will utter those ominous phrases "You probably can't read this, but..." or "I know this slide is very busy, but..."—and that wonderful little three-letter word provides justification for his going ahead with illegible or undecipherable material, and you are still expected to comprehend everything he says.

Brian's presentation included treatments of both the geological and geophysical studies that were under way, and he closed by discussing an integrated basin model that the team had developed using all of the available seismic and well data. Based on their visible reactions and the few questions they asked, Sam thought that Brian's presentation was well received by the partners, and he allowed himself a moment of personal pride in his role as one of the interpreters whose work was such an important element of the basin model.

As expected, the first of the two partner presentations was very short, largely because that company had a relatively small working interest in the concession and had effectively chosen to follow the lead of the concession operator (Sam's company). Unfortunately, the second partner presentation by Behemoth Oil, one of his company's staunchest competitors, turned out to be very different from what Sam had anticipated. He thought that there would be only a few minor disagreements between the two companies, ones that could be easily resolved in work sessions outside of formal technical meetings. This was not the case—the speaker for Behemoth, also an interpreter and a casual acquaintance of both Brian and Sam, was on the attack from the outset, questioning virtually every conclusion that Brian had put forward. What struck Sam was not so much the questioning of conclusions or techniques, but rather the speaker's language and aggressive manner, which seemed to intensify as the presentation ground on.

For some reason, this behavior was tolerated until the Behemoth geophysicist finally crossed the line. "These conclusions really come as no surprise, because this is what we've come to expect from the type of work that interpreters like Brian usually do."

Sam could hardly believe his ears. He had heard about the ad hominem method for advancing an argument but had never seen it in action. The speaker cast a hard look at Brian, who returned the glare but said nothing—at first. But the

> **When I was much younger, I once heard it said that you shouldn't criticize another geophysicist until you've interpreted 100 miles of his data.**

speaker continued to disparage the company's work, and by implication Brian's competence, and then Brian began to slowly get up from his chair. "Now wait just a minute here…" he said, and Sam, who was sitting next to Brian, thought for an instant that he might have to restrain him.

At this point, Paul intervened and called a break. The Behemoth interpreter hastily stepped out of the conference room, and Brian was able to calm down. When Paul reconvened the meeting, he moved directly to the commercial discussion, which lasted only 10 minutes, and then he adjourned the meeting. Brian and the Behemoth interpreter never looked at each other and left by separate doors.

As Sam was preparing to go, he noticed someone who apparently had stood silently in the back of the room throughout the entire meeting. He was Clark, one of the company's senior technical advisors, who had built his career and earned his reputation as a seismic interpreter. Apparently Paul had asked him to observe the meeting and then offer his assessment of the state of technical work for the concession. As Sam walked over to him, Clark was looking out of the window, his eyes focused on nothing in particular but his mind surely at work.

"What happened in here today, Clark? I've never seen anything like this before."

"What happened in here has happened before, too many times before, and probably will happen too many times again. It saddens me to think about it, more so to witness it. Of course you know that every profession has standards of behavior, and we are no exception. We follow a code of sorts, and that code says that you never attack another interpreter—even if he might have made a mistake (we've all done that), or because you have a legitimate difference of opinion with him, or because of some misplaced sense of loyalty to your own company. No, you don't attack another interpreter or his work because you can never be sure of the conditions or constraints under which he did it, and that uncertainty alone demands that he be given the chance to describe how and why he did what he did. When I was much younger, I once heard it said that you shouldn't criticize another geophysicist until you've interpreted 100 miles of his data."

Sam went home that day having learned an important lesson about interpretation that has nothing to do with geophysics.

> Now I hold it is not decent for a scientific gent
> To say another is an ass—at least, to all intent;
> Nor should the individual who happens to be meant
> Reply by heaving rocks at him, to any great extent.
>
> —Bret Harte

The best interpreter in the company

OCTOBER 2008

Dave, Sam's supervisor, called all of the geophysicists in his group to his office for a meeting to discuss plans for evaluating open acreage in preparation for an upcoming lease sale. The area involved in this sale was so large and covered by so many overlapping data sets that Dave had decided to split his staff into two teams, the first to do subregional interpretation and the second to follow closely behind with detailed prospect mapping of features identified by the first. Sam and the other interpreters thought that this approach would necessarily place the heavier burden on the shoulders of the first team, who would have to work quickly yet carefully through a lot of data in order to give the second team enough time to mature prospects for the sale. Sam secretly hoped to be named to the second team, guessing that its pace of work might not be so frantic, and also that an interpreter on that team was more likely to have the good fortune to map a prospect that might be bought, drilled, and eventually proven to be successful. Everyone knew that, among other things, Dave would reveal in this meeting whom he had selected for which team.

Dave wasted no time in dashing Sam's hopes when he was the first person named to the subregional team. After he had given assignments to all of his staff, Dave then informed the group that one more experienced interpreter, Steve, would be brought in from another department in the company to help out on the subregional team. Sam was surprised if not shocked when Dave said that Steve would have his own office and a technical assistant appointed to work exclusively for him. Dave correctly sensed the apprehension caused by his announcement of Steve's assignment and explained his reasons for adding him to the team.

"Most of you know Steve—he is very well regarded by everyone familiar with his work and is possibly the best interpreter in the company. I've asked him to join our subregional team because he can show us how to efficiently work through large volumes of data...."

Sam stopped listening after Dave referred to Steve as possibly "the best interpreter in the company." Although Sam knew Steve by reputation only and certainly not personally, he was offended by Dave's remark, questioning not only the basis for making such a judgment, but also Dave's repeating it explicitly to people whom he was supposed to lead and motivate. "The best interpreter in the company!" What do you mean by that? Measured how, and by whom? Has an opinion poll been taken, or did someone ace the test? What do you mean "best"—fastest, smartest, works longest hours, all of the above? Was he genetically engineered for maximum interpretive ability? Does he have one monstrous Cyclopean eye in the center of his forehead? Can he turn his head a full 270° like an owl? Can he make impossibly long jump correlations in a single bound? Does he accurately predict depths to formation tops to the nearest foot every time? Has he never used the delete key on his workstation?

What does that make the rest of us—second stringers, understudies, also-rans, wannabes?

> *Can he make impossibly long jump correlations in a single bound? Does he accurately predict depths to formation tops to the nearest foot every time? Has he never used the delete key on his workstation?*

Sam snapped out of his reverie in time to hear the last third of Dave's description of the schedule and major milestones for the project. Dave didn't ask if anyone had any questions, and so the meeting ended abruptly. Sam left the room and said nothing to anyone about working on the subregional team or with (or really for?) Steve—he felt it best to keep his thoughts to himself and let Dave's plan unfold as it might.

With little fanfare, Steve showed up in the office the following week and went to his private office where he kept pretty much to himself. Sam attended several meetings with Steve, at which he effectively presented his interpretations (although he never discussed his interpretive approach or any distinctive or innovative techniques he used), answered questions as they were put to him, and even asked a few questions of his own in return. The subregional team completed its evaluation on schedule and passed its work on to the prospect mapping team as planned, shortly after which Steve left the team as quietly and almost mysteriously as he had come. Sam noticed that there was nothing special about the form or manner in which Steve's work was documented, and there was no mention made of anything like "best practices" associated with his interpretive techniques, whatever they were.

In retrospect, Sam is a little disappointed that he didn't get to know Steve better, or for that matter, at all. Among other things, he wonders if Steve ever knew that Dave had spoken of him as "the best interpreter in the company." At the same time, Sam is glad to have had his experience with Steve on the subregional team because as a result he learned that no one is the best interpreter in his company. ▶

Epilogue

If J.R.R. Tolkien had been a seismic data processor

(A PREVIOUSLY UNPUBLISHED STORY WRITTEN IN 2008
FOR THE BROTHERHOOD OF SEISMIC DATA PROCESSORS)

Frodo took the flash drive from his pocket, where it was clasped to a lanyard that he often wore around his neck. He unfastened it and handed it slowly to the processor. It felt suddenly very heavy, as if either it or Frodo himself was in some way reluctant for the processor to handle it.

The processor held it up. It looked to be made of hard black plastic. "Can you see any markings on it?" he asked.

"None except the company logo," said Frodo. "It is quite plain, and it never shows a scratch or sign of wear."

"Well then, watch!" To Frodo's astonishment and distress the processor suddenly thrust the flash drive into a USB port on his PC. Frodo gave a cry and reached for the drive, but the processor held him back.

"Wait!" he said in a commanding voice, as he double-clicked on the 'My Computer' icon and started to download a file from the drive to his PC.

No apparent change came over the PC. After a few seconds the processor got up and closed the blinds at the window. His cubicle became darker and quieter, although Frodo could still hear the clicking of keyboards in adjacent cubicles. For a moment the processor stood looking at his monitor, then he sat down and clicked on the 'Safely Remove Hardware' icon on his PC.

"It is now safe to remove the device," said the processor. "Take it!" Frodo took it in his hand: It seemed to have become thicker and heavier than ever.

"Now look at the screen!" said the processor. "And look closely!"

As Frodo did so, he now saw many lines of code, completely filling the screen from top to bottom: lines of code that seemed to form the commands of a flowing script. They shone piercingly bright, and yet remote, as if out of a great depth of mathematical complexity.

"I cannot make any sense of this code," said Frodo in a quavering voice.

"No," said the processor, "but I can. The language is that of C++, which I will not speak further of here. But if you look at the comments, this in plain English is what is said, close enough:

Many CRPs in all, One Model to find them,
RTM to migrate all and in the image bind them.

It is only two lines of a verse long known in the lore of data processing:

Hallowed is the one true wave equation,
    In the art of seismic migration,
Whether by Kirchhoff summation,
    Or by downward continuation
In the Land of Processing where the Data lie.
    Many CRPs in all, One Model to find them,
    RTM to migrate all and in the image bind them
In the Land of Processing where the Data lie. ◗

Suggested Reading

Sam accepted the suggestion that he compile a list of the books and papers ("suggested reading" in *TLE* terminology) that over the years he has found to be most helpful to him as an interpreter. Following is that list, with apologies to authors to whom Sam is indebted but has not acknowledged here. Omitted from the list are numerous references to nonearth-science volumes that have assisted Sam in getting along in business and in life and have contributed meaningfully to the personal philosophy he has brought to his work. If Sam's list appears somewhat short, keep in mind two admonitions offered by C. H. Dix in his classic 1952 book (my italics):

The general problem of picking [interpreting] reflections is, of course, extremely important. It is also one that is somewhat *difficult to describe*.

And later in that same text:

Where the correlation of one reflection record with another [interpretation] is very easy, little needs to be said. Almost anyone can understand such a correlation. On the other hand, this is a rare occurrence. The usual thing is for the correlation to be so difficult as to be impossible. It is for this reason that correlation procedure *can hardly be described in words*.

Who knows what he might have said if he had commented a third time. Worth mentioning in this context is a statement that Dix made in an interview with Dean Clark published in *TLE* in August 1984:

It's important to have someone look at things as simply as possible to get as broad a picture as possible. There's a lot to be said for simplicity; it lets you appreciate what you're doing, you get a feel for it. But today, the person who does the final interpretation often doesn't have a feel for the particular area because he often has no contact with the field and doesn't know what processing was done or why certain processing was done.

My feeling all along has been that you should get along with as little as possible of the fancy methods. After all, the earth is a nonhomogeneous mess and no matter how hard you try not to smooth it out or idealize it in your processing, you have to do some of that. So eventually you're going to have to use your instinct. That's why it's critical to develop a feel for these things.

Books

Brown, A. R., 2002, Interpretation of three-dimensional seismic data, sixth edition: AAPG Memoir 42. *(Because this book currently is in its sixth edition, Sam is mildly embarrassed to admit that his copy is only the third edition.)*

Dix, C. H., 1952, Seismic prospecting for oil, first edition: Harper & Row. *(The second edition of this book was published by IHRDC in 1981.)*

Sheriff, R. E., 2002, Encyclopedic dictionary of applied geophysics, fourth edition: SEG.
Tucker, P. M., and H. J. Yorston, 1973, Pitfalls in seismic interpretation: SEG.
Yilmaz, O., 2001, Seismic data analysis: Processing, inversion, and interpretation of seismic data: SEG.

Papers
Castagna, J. P. and H. W. Swan, 1997, Principles of AVO crossplotting: The Leading Edge, **16**, 337–342.
Connolly, P., 1999, Elastic impedance: The Leading Edge, **18**, 438–452.
Kaufman, H., 1953, Velocity functions in seismic prospecting: Geophysics, **18**, 289–297.
Ostrander, W. J., 1984, Plane-wave reflection coefficients for gas sands at nonnormal angles of incidence: Geophysics, **49**, 1637–1648.
Russell, B., 1998, A simple seismic imaging exercise: The Leading Edge, **17**, 885–889.
Tucker, P., 1988, Seismic contouring: A unique skill: Geophysics, **53**, 741–749.
Widess, M. B., 1973, How thin is a thin bed: Geophysics, **38**, 1176–1180.

The papers by Russell and Tucker are two of Sam's all-time practical favorites. The latter paper is especially so because it calls to attention the skills involved in the lost art of contouring, which has been replaced by the mechanical selection of parameters for gridding and contouring algorithms—which almost always include a smoothing operation of some kind. In the bad old days an interpreter would have smoothed his or her map as a fundamental component of contouring, incorporating an admittedly subjective feel for both data quality and geologic style.

And in general
Case histories (e.g., most recently Johnson et al., 2007, Covenant field: A major oil discovery in the Sevier thrust belt of central Utah: The Leading Edge, **26**, 168–171). *(Sam thinks that SEG can certainly use as many papers like this as it can get.)*
Papers dealing specifically with interpretation techniques (e.g., most recently Reasnor, M. D., 2007, Salt interpretation practices for depth imaging in the Gulf of Mexico: The Leading Edge, **26**, 1438–1441). *(Sam especially appreciates authors who have taken the time to write papers about interpretation techniques that many people either take for granted or are not permitted to discuss in a public forum.)*
Papers on pitfalls in seismic interpretation (from Sam's own publications, of which there aren't many, the one titled "Problems with too much data" (The Leading Edge, **20**, 1124–1126) was the most fun to write—it contains only two figures and not a single equation). *(Sam figures that there aren't very many of these papers because people are either uncomfortable or forbidden to talk about their mistakes in public. To do so can be perceived alternatively as admission of error (bad) or as springboard to discovery (good); in either case, one won't quickly or easily gain permission to release data and information relating to them.)*

As a final comment Sam takes note of two of the more memorable examples of colorful language that he's found in geophysical publications, having always thought that geophysicists should seek opportunities to enliven their writing and add color to more than just the frequency content of their data. His favorites are, as you might expect, Dix's *threshold of impossibility* as the point beyond which each individual interpreter in view of his own limitations should correlate no farther, and Tucker's *limit-of-trivia* as a description of the noise in data that should not be rigorously honored during contouring. There probably are more and better examples of the power of descriptive language to be found in our wealth of published geophysical data and information, and Sam remains vigilant in looking for them. ❧